"Common grace theology has been a necessary reminder that God is at work promoting signs of truth, goodness, and beauty beyond the boundaries of the redeemed community. Now in this fine book Tim Muehlhoff not only adds significant insights to that exploration but he also brings it into new territory, focusing on the reach of God's healing power into communities of grieving, abused, and oppressed human beings."

Richard J. Mouw, president emeritus of Fuller Theological Seminary

"The word *gospel* literally means 'good news.' But much of the news proclaimed by Christians today doesn't sound too good. In fact, for many hearers, the news sounds caustic and divisive. Why? Because the gospel message has been co-opted by words that have either lost their meaning or changed over time in the ebb and flow of a fickle culture. Tim Muehlhoff's book *Eyes to See* invites us to step back to take a fresh look at the goodness and beauty in the world, compelling the seeker to trace their natural attraction to its source. We have more that unites us than divides us. Helping others understand common grace is the God-honoring way to proclaim the gospel today. This book is a must-read."

Harry Edwards, founder and director of Apologetics.com

"Some refer to it as a happy accident, others as good luck, and still many others as just a coincidence. The truth is that God's grace through faith exists in every cell of the universe, and we are its blind recipients. Tim Muehlhoff has been a strong presence on our radio show for over a decade. His deep dive for our listeners into vexing and mysterious theological topics delivered with great whimsy is always a show highlight. In *Eyes to See,* Tim opens our eyes to the miracle of God's great gift of grace. As he is on air so he is in print—thoughtful, generous, and always Christ affirming."

John Hall, radio host on WORD-FM, Pittsburgh

"Have you ever wondered where God is in the things that are happening around you? Then you need this book. It will sensitize your eyes, your ears, and your heart to find God in the often-missed places where he is at work every day. Tim's concrete examples are helpful not just for personal understanding, but they also can be shared with others who are wondering where God is in the midst of the times we are living in."

Katie Potesta, adult fellowships shepherd at Fullerton Free Church

"The apostle Paul said a defining characteristic of human beings toward God is ingratitude. This book helps correct that leaning. Muehlhoff does a great job helping us see and explain that God's great kindness abounds everywhere."

Ben and Janet Burns, Cru City, marriage and family educators

"The idea of common grace has long captured the imagination of Dr. Tim Muehlhoff—the idea of blessing and provision and healing that might not appear miraculous but more common and experienced by all, believer and unbeliever, every day. He constantly reminds those around him to be alert to it, watch for it, celebrate it, and recount the stories of it. This common grace is at its core truly anything *but* common in that it reflects the daily, hourly, moment-by-small-moment intersections of sinful man with almighty God—enough in itself to blow our minds."

Jenni Key, shepherd of prayer at Fullerton Free Church and chair of the board of directors, Evangelical Free Church of America

"Dr. Muehlhoff's latest book, *Eyes to See*, is a sure jolt of encouragement for anyone who needs it—and I'm pretty sure that is me and everyone I know. Using his mastery of brilliant written illustrations, Muehlhoff helps us all to see the supernatural hand of God moving mightily in the seemingly unexceptional aspects of our daily lives. It would be hard to find a better book to read through with a small group in your church—or for that matter, the whole congregation. This book is in the truest sense of the words an eye-opening experience that will boost the faith of its readers measurably."

Craig J. Hazen, founder and director of the Christian apologetics program at Biola University and author of *Fearless Prayer*

"If you're wondering whether God is doing much of anything in our world, we urge you to read this probing book! In *Eyes to See*, Tim Muehlhoff makes a convincing case for a God who is intricately involved in the big and small of our lives through a means called common grace. Tim, a masterful storyteller and pop-culture enthusiast, will surprise, inspire, inform, and reassure you that God's influence actually saturates our lives in ways we may never have considered, even in these dark days of our history."

David and Beth Booram, cofounders and directors of Fall Creek Abbey, authors of *When Faith Becomes Sight*

"Ever wonder why God isn't more active in the world today? In *Eyes to See*, Tim Muehlhoff suggests that God *is* active but that we're unaccustomed to seeing it. This fascinating book helps us see that God works in all sorts of recognizable ways if we willing to see his 'ordinary' acts in the world."

Sean McDowell, associate professor of Christian apologetics at Biola University and coauthor of *Evidence That Demands a Verdict*

"Tim Muehlhoff has one of the sharpest-yet-grace-giving minds that we know. Everything he writes will challenge and sharpen you, but with a freedom that brings out the best in you. This book will open your eyes to the majesty of God that is all around us and yet we often miss. Not only will this book give you 'ears to hear' but now 'eyes to see.'"

Dave and Ann Wilson, hosts of *Family Life Today*

"Tim Muehlhoff's *Eyes to See* brings the topic of common grace to the fore in fresh and compelling ways. Tim helps his readers understand and embrace God's common grace by asking and answering some of today's most pertinent questions and provides a host of examples for initiating meaningful conversations. I especially appreciate how each chapter includes resources for readers who want to dig deeper. I highly recommend *Eyes to See* as an engaging read and excellent resource."

Cas Monaco, executive director of Cru

"In a most engaging way, Tim Muehlhoff's *Eyes to See* will move you toward greater wonder or cause you to wonder more, or both."

Joanne Jung, professor of biblical and theological studies at Biola University

"What a timely resource for a world wondering where God is! Tim's book is a refreshing reminder that God is always at work and always speaking, if only we would pay attention and have eyes to see and ears to hear. It's time to be encouraged!"

John and Missy Maurer, Baylor sports ministry

"In *Eyes to See*, Tim Muehlhoff provides insight and practical application for the common grace from God that is relevant to every age and generation."

Scott Ricketson, biker chaplain for Orange County

"Having trouble seeing God these days? You're not alone. In the midst of hardship and doubt, it's easy to lose sight of God and subsequently our hope. *Eyes to See* is an engaging and honest book. It brings God back into focus in the everyday challenges and questions of life so that we can see hope and help restore it for others."

Andy Steiger, president of Apologetics Canada and author of *Reclaimed*

TIM MUEHLHOFF

FOREWORD BY
J. P. MORELAND

Eyes
to
See

RECOGNIZING
GOD'S COMMON GRACE
IN AN UNSETTLED
WORLD

An imprint of InterVarsity Press
Downers Grove, Illinois

InterVarsity Press
P.O. Box 1400, Downers Grove, IL 60515-1426
ivpress.com
email@ivpress.com

InterVarsity Press® is the book-publishing division of InterVarsity Christian Fellowship/USA®, a
movement of students and faculty active on campus at hundreds of universities, colleges, and
schools of nursing in the United States of America, and a member movement of the International
Fellowship of Evangelical Students. For information about local and regional activities,
visit intervarsity.org.

All Scripture quotations, unless otherwise indicated, are taken from The Holy Bible, New
International Version®, NIV®. Copyright © 1973, 1978, 1984, 2011 by Biblica, Inc.™ Used by
permission of Zondervan. All rights reserved worldwide. www.zondervan.com. The "NIV" and
"New International Version" are trademarks registered in the United States Patent and Trademark
Office by Biblica, Inc.™

While any stories in this book are true, some names and identifying information may have been
changed to protect the privacy of individuals.

Cover design and image composite: David Fassett
Interior design: Jeanna Wiggins
Images: green plant: © heibaihui / iStock / Getty Images Plus
        purple flowers: © Nares Chaladkit / EyeEm / Getty Images
        grass growing up through concrete: © Valerii Maksimov / iStock / Getty Images Plus

ISBN 978-0-8308-3165-4 (print)
ISBN 978-0-8308-3166-1 (digital)

Library of Congress Cataloging-in-Publication Data

Names: Muehlhoff, Tim, 1961– author.
Title: Eyes to see: recognizing God's common grace in an unsettled world /
    Tim Muehlhoff; foreword by J.P. Moreland.
Description: Downers Grove. IL: InterVarsity Press, [2021] | Includes
    bibliographical references.
Identifiers: LCCN 2021034707 (print) | LCCN 2021034708 (ebook) | ISBN
    9780830831654 (print) | ISBN 9780830831661 (digital)
Subjects: LCSH: Grace (Theology)
Classification: LCC BT761.3 .M84 2021 (print) | LCC BT761.3 (ebook) | DDC
    234—dc23
LC record available at https://lccn.loc.gov/2021034707
LC ebook record available at https://lccn.loc.gov/2021034708

P 25 24 23 22 21 20 19 18 17 16 15 14 13 12 11 10 9 8 7 6 5 4 3 2 1
Y 37 36 35 34 33 32 31 30 29 28 27 26 25 24 23 22 21

TO OUR SMALL GROUP—

Jon, Pam, Dave, Debbie, Chris, Alisa, Rick,
Sherri, Doug, Deb, Gregg, Jeannie—

*who during a pandemic showed
my wife (Noreen) and me what common grace
looks like in action. Our laughter, tears, gifts, prayers,
and endless Zoom meetings spurred me on to
see God faithfully at work in a suddenly
unsettled world.*

Contents

Foreword

J. P. Moreland

Ideas matter.

In fact, we are largely at the mercy of the ideas we embrace. They provide the conscious, sometimes subconscious, rails on which we live our lives. But this obvious truth raises an equally obvious problem: How can we ensure that we embrace the true, rational, biblical, life-giving ideas and reject their opposites? This problem is exacerbated by the simple fact that unless we follow the early Christian mystics and live in caves far away from civilization, we live, move, and have our being in a culture. And it is a difficult task to navigate our lives so we "don't let the world around [us] squeeze [us] into its mold" (Rom 12:2 Phillips). Like it or not, our thought lives are a battlefield.

Never in the history of Western culture has this life-or-death struggle been more subtle yet severe. As the West slouched toward secularism, we have lost—*lost*—a biblically supernatural view of the world, a perspective that would sustain and strengthen us graciously to stand firm against the tide washing over us. But we are so often adrift, cut loose from our source of power, unable to see God's miraculous partnership with us in these unsettling times.

That's the bad news. Here's the good news. There is a way out of the situation, a way of finding the anchor for our souls that we have temporarily lost. This way requires us to rediscover and come to know—not just believe in but know—that the supernatural world is real and God is acting with and for us all the time. I believe there are two equally important and complementary ways of recapturing what we have lost. The first strategy involves making it evident that dramatic, miraculous interventions from God are happening around us all the time, but we seldom hear credible accounts of these events. This is the approach I have taken in my book *A Simple Guide to Experiencing Miracles*. As I was writing that book, I was in communication with Tim Muehlhoff about the second strategy he was taking, an approach that I take to be even more fundamental than mine.

Muehlhoff's strategy is the central core of *Eyes to See*: providing us with the tools needed to be alerted to see and profit from recognizing cases of God's intervention in the so-called less dramatic "ordinary" events of daily life. It would be a shame—and profoundly unbiblical—if we saw God's actions only in the dramatic events. Such a limited perspective leaves out the awareness of what God is doing in the more ordinary course of events. Muehlhoff solves this problem in a way that makes this book a must-read. We don't want to take the ordinary course of events as occasions to blindly see them as divine orchestrations "through the eyes of faith." No, we need to be given reasons for taking them in this way. We need tools and specific examples that help us develop steady convictions about this way of seeing. I can't think of a better book that addresses these issues than *Eyes to See*.

Tim Muehlhoff is a colleague and friend. I have known this brother for several decades and cowrote an apologetics book with him, *The God Conversation: Using Stories and Illustrations to Explain Your Faith*. There are many reasons why I admire him, but one stands out, not because it is the most important thing about him but because it is so rare and needed in the body of Christ: Tim always comes up with a fresh, neglected, and important way of looking at something so many others, including me, don't see. As a result I have learned from him to put on a new set of glasses or been challenged to dust off an old set that I have failed to wear for a long time. In this way, Tim has regularly enriched my life, broadened and deepened my love for Jesus, and facilitated my growth toward a mature, healthy Jesus follower.

Among his many important books, *Eyes to See* may just be at the top of the list. Its publication is exactly for such a time as this.

Introduction

LOOKING FOR GOD

Which would you pick?

If you could travel back to biblical times to witness God in action, what would you *most* want to see? Imagine the possibilities. You shield yourself from the spray as Pharaoh's chariots are consumed by raging waters. Trumpets blast as the seemingly impenetrable walls of Jericho fall with a deafening thud, shaking the ground beneath you. Your hair is singed as fire comes down from heaven consuming the prophet Elijah's sacrifice as hundreds of Baal's prophets are silenced. Or perhaps you'd opt for watching Jesus heal the leper, raise Lazarus, or feed the five thousand.

How many would choose to watch early Christians collect food for the poor, help build sanitation systems for the city of Antioch, or provide life-saving assistance to Roman citizens during a plague in AD 165?

The goal of *Eyes to See* is to expand our view of what counts as an act of God, realizing that the ingenuity of designing a sanitation system and parting the sea are both divine. In no way am I discounting the dramatic acts of God that are the topic of movies or sermons. Nor am I suggesting that God doesn't act in miraculous ways today—reports from missionaries abroad record miracles too many to ignore, and many of us have answers to prayer that defy natural explanations. Rather, I'm attempting to bring attention to an oft-forgotten avenue of divine action called *common grace*, where God indiscriminately provides blessings to a rebellious world. If miraculous acts are God's highlight reel, then common grace is the ever-present but oft-ignored elevator music that plays in the background of our lives 24/7.

Our desire for the dramatic is understandable and perhaps stoked by some of our favorite worship songs. In the rousing song "Rattle!" we hear: "My God is able to save and deliver and heal and restore anything that He wants to."[1] In another song, "Famous For,"[2] a person longs to have experiences on par with a lion's mouth's being closed, standing in fire, and walking through the waters. The lyrics reference powerful moments such as Daniel being thrown in a den of lions but not being eaten (Dan 6); Shadrach, Meshach, and Abednego surviving the king's furnace (Dan 3); and the parting of the Red Sea (Ex 14).

Putting these two songs together, we learn God can do *anything*—heal, deliver, restore—he wants to, and he's done it in the past as evidenced by lions' mouths being closed. So, why doesn't he heal or deliver more often? Serving as an interim teaching pastor at a church in Orange County, California, I had many people come up after a stirring sermon or worship set and ask in hushed tones, "Why doesn't God answer my prayers? We are desperate and he doesn't seem to be doing anything!"

There is no doubt that the dramatic stories and miracles in the Bible, sermons, and worship songs are praiseworthy and faith-building, but shouldn't God be equally famous for less dramatic acts that improve our lives? As we shall see, God is praiseworthy for medical discoveries, technological advancement, and community building via common grace. When we begin to acknowledge God's common grace we'll soon see he longs to help with our problems and is active in dramatic answers to prayer *and* in the aspirin we take for a blistering headache and the church benevolence fund that helps in hard times.

Common Grace

We can think of common grace as *the generous blessings God pours out on the entire human race without discrimination or bias*. The psalmist proclaims to a world in rebellion that the "Lord is good to all" and has "compassion on all he has made" (Ps 145:9).

What is the good we experience? Jesus offers one example when he states that God makes "his sun rise on the evil and on the good, and sends rain on the just and the unjust" (Mt 5:45 ESV). Paul reiterates this point when he informs unbelievers at Lystra that God is the one who sends "rains from heaven and fruitful seasons" (Acts 14:17 ESV). After the fall, the earth didn't produce only thorns or thistles, but equally plush vineyards, crops, oceans teeming with a myriad of fish, and minerals buried in the ground.

The central feature of this type of grace is that *all* people experience it. Rebels and saints alike can count on regular seasons to plant and harvest crops, learn to build fires for cold nights, create language to communicate with others, discover medicines to fight off disease, formulate governments to help communities flourish, navigate long journeys by consulting the stars, learn the truths of mathematics for abstract thinking, and create art to imagine beauty and draw us up to higher ideals.

Common Grace and Suffering

The doctrine of common grace is particularly relevant when we and those we care about face hardship. When we encounter racism or sexism, a pandemic, or personal tragedy, we desire God to show himself. During these times, Christians and non-Christians alike ironically utter the same refrain: *Where is God?* Comedian and film director Woody Allen once quipped that if God exists he's certainly an underachiever. Sting, the former front man for the rock group The Police, laments in a haunting song that if Jesus is alive, "then how come he never lives here?"[3]

If God exists, asks a skeptical friend, then where in the world is he? Why doesn't he show himself? That is the question we'll be answering in this book—*What constitutes God acting in a world of pain and turmoil?* If we have a limited idea of what divine action looks like—dramatic answers to prayer, healings with no medical explanation, financial needs being met unexpectedly by total strangers—then we have lessened the power of common grace exhibited by antibiotics, financial planners, and thoughtful friends.

The story of Matt Hughes offers an example of how common grace works. Fans of the Ultimate Fighting Championship (UFC) know the key role Hughes played in the success of mixed martial arts. Today, the UFC is appraised as a five-billion-dollar organization and oversees one of the fastest-growing sports in the world. Inducted into the UFC Hall of Fame, Matt almost didn't see the meteoric rise of his sport. On June 18, 2017, his truck was hit by a northbound train resulting in severe brain and physical injuries. Today, Matt has made a remarkable recovery due to a multitude of factors. He explains, "I am beyond grateful for every physician, doctor, nurse, therapist, coach, first responder, family member, friend, etc. who worked with me over the past 3 years. I thank God for guiding their hands and their decisions."[4]

Could God have miraculously saved Matt from the train wreck? After the accident, could God have instantaneously healed him? Yes, to both. God can do "immeasurably more than all we ask or imagine" (Eph 3:20). But any Christian will tell you that dramatic prayers often don't get answered as we hoped. Is it any less an act of God that Matt's recovery came through God guiding the hands of doctors, physical therapists, and family members? The goal of *Eyes to See* is to give you illustrations that widen what it means for God to address our pain.

The premise of this book is founded on two claims. First, God is aware of not only what is currently happening but what will happen. God fully knew what would happen to Matt on June 18, 2017. However, God's knowledge that an event will occur does not *cause* it to happen. Rather, his knowledge is all-inclusive —past, present, and future. For example, did God know Adam and Eve would eventually rebel by eating from the Tree of the Knowledge of Good and Evil? Yes. But he's not responsible for their rebellion; he simply knew what the first humans would freely do in the garden. The New Testament author James affirms this when he reminds us that when we are tempted to sin, we should not blame God because he "cannot be tempted by evil, nor does he tempt anyone" (Jas 1:13).

There are two ways I can know what's in a particular book. First, I could know what's in each chapter because I'm the author and I wrote it. I control the actions of each character and the twists and turns of the plot. On the other hand, I could know what happens in each chapter because I've read the entire book cover to cover. I don't control the characters but am aware of their actions. My argument is that God is like the latter. He knows the future because he is the Alpha and Omega, the Beginning and the End (Rev 21:6).

The second claim is that via foreknowledge God knows what challenges humans will face in a rebellious world—disease, famine, war, pandemics, global warming, and AIDS, to name a few. Subsequently, he strategically gives us gifts—scientific discoveries, agriculture, antibiotics, ethics—that help us not only survive but thrive. These gifts are given in partnership with us and constitute common grace.

In an unsettled world, the doctrine of common grace can bring great comfort knowing that rather than abandoning us, God continually guides us in how to navigate a fallen world. The genesis of this book occurred while waiting with my wife for her to have a body scan to see if her cancer had metastasized. It was a scary time, and I remember thinking how thankful I was for a lab tech who has spent her life gaining the skill to operate a multimillion-dollar machine that will search every inch of my wife's body looking for cancer. "Thank God for this hospital and that machine," I blurted out to my wife. She squeezed my hand and agreed.

I then realized how little I do that: give God credit for things taken for granted. Yes, I desperately wanted God to miraculously take my wife's cancer away. He didn't. But he did give us doctors, lab technicians, diagnostic machines, compassionate nurses, and ultimately a procedure performed by the only specialist in the area qualified to do so; through these God took away all the cancer.

As Christians called to be God's spokespeople it's not enough to merely understand the workings of common grace. Rather, we are compelled to communicate God's care to a world in disarray. One key component is to offer friends, coworkers, and family members vivid and memorable illustrations of common grace.

The Lasting Power of Illustrations

Once a conversation is over, how much does a person remember? Based on what researchers call "the forgetting curve" a day or two later you retain only 40 percent. In another few days you'll most likely have forgotten everything unless there is something within the conversation that stands out and is memorable.[5] Illustrations and examples have a staying power and make up a large part of what a person remembers long after the conversation has ended.

The goal of this book is twofold. First, to understand and embrace the doctrine of common grace. What does it mean that all good gifts come from God (Jas 1:17)? Second, to learn to recognize these good gifts in daily life and illustrate them to the people around us. Once understood, illustrations of common grace will become apparent in the Netflix series we can't stop watching, novels we can't put down, scientific discoveries, history of inventions, and so forth.

"Once a wise saying is driven into the mind," suggests theologian Philip Ryken, "it stays there, like a nail pounded into a block of wood."[6] I hope that the stories, quotes, and examples you read in the following pages will help you create your own illustrations that, like a nail pounded into wood, will have staying power with those who need to hear of God's enduring concern and care.

Unique Features of the Book

Eyes to See is laid out in a format that makes it helpful to those wanting to communicate the Christian perspective to others.

Using pop culture as a conversation starter. My students tell me the greatest hindrance to talking with their friends about God is not knowing how to start the conversation. "God just never seems to come up" is a constant refrain. I ask them if they talk about the newest Netflix series or current events like Covid-19. Christian communicators need to be adept at finding the spiritual truths embedded in *The Tiger King* or issues dominating the headlines. The great traveling preacher John Wesley maintained that a Christian should be able to relate every story on the front page of a newspaper to the gospel. This book offers examples of how to start conversations revolving around daily topics or movies in your Hulu queue.

Common objections. Authentic conversations involve a give-and-take process in which our skeptical friends get to ask questions and even offer objections. These objections should be taken seriously. "To answer before listening," suggest the ancient writers that comprise the book of Proverbs, "that is folly and shame" (Prov 18:13). Each chapter includes legitimate objections and possible responses.

Going deeper. *Eyes to See* is written for readers who have little background in Christian apologetics. For those who want more, "Going Deeper" sections offer a richer examination of topics and are found throughout the chapters. These sections may not be the kind of material you would bring into a conversation, but they offer valuable context.

Diverse illustrations. In addition to my own original stories and illustrations, you'll encounter thought-provoking illustrations from noted thinkers such as C. S. Lewis, Tim Keller, Augustine, Maria Lugones, Camus, Aristotle, Betty Friedan, Bruce Lee, and others.

A quick word about the topics covered in this book. When researching common grace, many theologians mention categories such as reliable seasons for agriculture, a moral conscience, ability to reason, creation of institutions, and the creative realm. While I cover many of these areas, I want to ask questions that explore aspects of common grace that I—and hopefully you—will find interesting. How might our immune systems relate to God's sense of social justice? Can art help us question the damaging narratives we get from pop culture concerning romantic love and an identity built on status and possessions? In today's argument culture, does common grace give us a vision for how words can both hurt and heal? As acts of violence dominate headlines, does God help us mitigate the effects of it through organizations such as the Red Cross and the emergence of humane self-defense systems? How does common grace change how we view God's response to pain and suffering? I hope you'll not only find answers that are stimulating but also ones that broaden our concept of common grace.

Wishing It Were True

For Christians, God is the great comforter who views us with tender loving-kindness. "As a father has compassion on his children," states the psalmist, "so the LORD has compassion on those who fear him" (Ps 103:13). However, not everyone sees God in that way. Noted atheist Sam Harris boldly states that "Everyone who has eyes to see can see that if the God of Abraham exists, He is an utter psychopath."[7] While most people are not that brazenly disparaging of God, they may view him very differently from you. What's to be done?

Blaise Pascal, a radical follower of Jesus during the 1600s, wrote copious notes to himself exploring how to present the Christian perspective to his non-Christian friends. One note reads, "Next, make it [Christianity] attractive, make good men wish it were true, and then show that it is."[8] Wouldn't it be comforting to your friends to know in a world of disease, hardship, and environmental challenges that God from the very beginning has been providing us with medical discoveries, technological breakthroughs, psychological insights, and conceptions of virtuous love? We are not left alone to face life's challenges. Could it possibly be true?

In her haunting poem "Nothing," Krysten Hill writes that when life is too much "I imagine a god / up there to fill what seems unimaginable."[9] As Christians, we can help people like Hill envision the benevolent God of the Scriptures who isn't "up there" but rather *here* working among us. In the pages to follow, we'll encounter a compassionate God who partners with us in a world of turmoil. This is a view of divine love expressed through common grace that our friends will, hopefully, long to be true.

CHAPTER ONE

Common Grace

GOD IN ACTION

"Houston, we have a problem."[1]

Not the words you want to utter when you're 205,000 miles from Earth. While performing a daily task—stirring oxygen tanks—the crew of Apollo 13 hears a bang that shakes the entire space rocket. The crew learns they are rapidly losing oxygen and have lost the ability to maneuver their craft. A worst-case scenario comes true!

The good news is that the bang is also heard by Mission Control in Houston, Texas, which carefully monitors every step of the flight. Immediately, the best of the best spring into action. Technicians begin complex problem solving, while test pilots jump into flight simulators to figure out how to navigate a damaged rocket back home. Psychologists, doctors, and priests check in regularly to help the stranded astronauts cope. The rest is history as Apollo 13 eventually lands safely in the South Pacific Ocean at 12:07 p.m. (CST) on April 17, 1970. A tragedy averted.

Imagine Mission Control didn't exist: the three crew members are left to figure it out themselves. No outside help or guidance. Alone. There's little doubt the story of Apollo 13 would have ended tragically without the guidance of Mission Control. Gladly, that wasn't the case. We encounter the same good news with the doctrine of common grace, which argues that God is figuratively humanity's Mission Control. As we face hardship, God not only monitors our situation but helps us. God— eminently wiser than NASA experts—is not only aware of the struggles of our wayward planet but actively works with us to cope.

I used the above illustration to conclude a talk to an adult fellowship group at my church. A week later I received an email from a woman who said she couldn't stop thinking about my illustration. "To be honest, I'm jealous of Mission Control." She explained that at least the stranded astronauts could directly talk to experts on the ground resulting in a two-way conversation. "I pray and get nothing from God. I'm pretty much ready to give up."

I resonated with her frustration. During the entire ordeal, NASA had *direct* contact with the crew of Apollo 13. Through sophisticated communication links, the three-man crew could directly converse with experts in Houston. Not so with God. His interaction is often indirect and not always easily detected. The result is that during trying times, we—like this woman who emailed me—often find ourselves doubting God.

I shared with this woman that many of the giants of the faith have equally wrestled with this issue and longed for God to definitively show himself. One of those was Blaise Pascal, who in the 1600s wrote a thought-provoking exploration of faith titled *Pensées*. In this series of notes, he gives voice to the frustration that God could, if he wanted, remove all doubt and reveal himself. With frustration apparent, Pascal longs for God to either put up or shut up.

> I am in a pitiful state. I have wished a hundred times over that, if there is a God supporting nature, she should unequivocally proclaim him, and that, if the signs in nature are deceptive, they should be completely erased; that nature should say all or nothing, so that I could see what course I ought to follow.[2]

I deeply resonate with Pascal's desire that God gives us an undeniable sign he exists and is ready to intervene during times of turmoil.

Ironically, it's not just believers who long for an unequivocal sign that God is real. Often, those outside the Christian community also long for God to show himself during hard times. In autumn 2020 when Covid rates were spiking and the news was dominated with dire stories, I mentioned to a non-Christian friend that I was preaching via Zoom at my church. He asked what I was speaking on. "God's faithfulness in hard times," I responded. "Good luck with that," he said laughing.

He didn't mean to offend, but his laugh spoke volumes and reminded me how odd my faith must seem to him at times. A pandemic rages and I still want to argue that God is not asleep at the wheel but is attentive to the needs of a world seemingly spinning out of control. I get his skepticism. Rather than getting defensive, I decided to continue the conversation by telling him that I often feel like a character from my favorite television show—*The Walking Dead*.

FAITH DURING A ZOMBIE APOCALYPSE

Depending on what metrics you use, *The Walking Dead* may have been *the* most-watched show on television—period. With strong global viewership, millions tuned in to see how a ragtag group of human survivors face an ever-increasing zombie uprising. Be warned, the show is graphic and emotionally grim. Yet, amid such gore one character, Hershel Greene, surprisingly starts each morning by reading his King James Bible and praying. "Surprised you still do that," sarcastically notes another survivor. He's got a point—with a world in disarray how can faith survive? If ever there was a time for God to show up and intervene, it would be now. Yet clues of God's activity are hard to come by. Still, Hershel feels compelled by his faith to help others. "Now, I can make these people feel better and hang on a little bit longer. I can save lives. And that's enough reason to risk mine," he informs his concerned daughter.[3]

I most relate to Hershel when hard times hit, a loved one suffers through seemingly never-ending cancer treatments, or finances are shredded by an unexpected pandemic. But like Hershel I'm still compelled by faith to continue on. What has most fueled my faith is changing my idea of what it means for God to show up during hard times.

What Does It Mean for God to Show Up?

Expectations play a key role in shaping our perspective. How do you expect a spouse or child to act toward you? What expectations do you have for your boss or coworkers? Unmet expectations can dramatically affect any relationship. The same is true with

God. How do we expect him to answer prayer or to come to our aid in time of need? Jewish theologian Martin Buber speculated that God often seems silent and distant because we expect that he'd always communicate to us in dramatic ways, such as a thunderclap or undeniable epiphany—"Thus saith the Lord!"[4] When we long for God to act, is that what we envision? Before we can talk to our non-Christian friends about God's response to a world in turmoil, we have to determine how we envision God responding. Do we expect answers to prayer to be dramatic and undeniable or subtle? The answer to this question will determine whether our faith flourishes during hard times or falters.

One way I've found it helpful to surface expectations—of both Christians and non-Christians—is to share an old joke.

FLASH FLOODS, ROWBOATS, OR GOD

An emergency announcement breaks radio programing. A flash flood is imminent and residents are to seek higher ground. A God-fearing man ignores the report, "I have nothing to worry about; God will save me!" As the flood water rises, he finds himself looking out a second-floor window as a rescue boat floats past his house and the captain says, "Get into the boat, we have room!" He waves them on, confident God will save him. As the waters rise, he takes refuge on the roof as a FEMA helicopter flies over and a rescue worker shouts, "We are here to help! Take hold of the ladder!" Again, he waves them on, assured God will come through. Eventually, he drowns and stands before God. "Why didn't you help me?" the man asks in an angry tone. God responds, "What more did you want? I sent you a radio warning, a boat, and a helicopter!"

We ignore God's common provisions due to an expectation of the supernatural. If you were the man stuck on a rooftop surrounded by flood waters, what would you expect divine intervention to look like? Do you imagine supernatural crosswinds parting the water around your house, or do you accept a helicopter as an act of God? Can't God do both? Yes, there is plenty of scriptural evidence of God parting seas, performing miraculous healings, and feeding thousands from a few loaves of bread. But should that be our expectation of how God will *regularly* act? My experience is that dramatic or overtly supernatural answers to prayer are few and far between. Does that mean God is delinquent or immune to our pleas for help? No. It may mean that our expectations of God are blinding us to more subtle ways he acts. The man on the roof brushes off a radio warning, a rescue boat, and a helicopter as he seeks the supernatural. But is such a view too limiting? Can't a radio message, brave rescue workers in a boat, or a FEMA helicopter count as God's intervention? Consider the curious—and perhaps divine—genesis of the idea of a helicopter.

A FLYING BOAT BECOMES REALITY

In his dream he's walking down a narrow passageway filled with elaborate doors. Suddenly, a strong vibration lifts his feet from the ground. The boy is carried straight up in a marvelous flying boat. Who knew the dream of an eleven-year-old Igor Sikorsky—secluded in Kiev, Ukraine—would eventually make aviation history with the creation of the modern helicopter? Sikorsky couldn't shake the dream, and by age twelve he was designing complex models of his flying boat. He desired to create a flying machine that would help save people in difficult-to-reach areas. After moving to America, Sikorsky, now an adult, founded the Sikorsky Aero Engineering Corp. and designed the VS-300 helicopter in 1939. To him flying a helicopter "is like a dream to feel the machine lift you gently up in the air, float smoothly over one spot for indefinite periods, move up or down under good control, as well as move not only forward or backward but in any direction."[5] His desire to help people also became a reality. Each year his company gives out awards to pilots who rescue people in Sikorsky helicopters. According to pilot self-reporting, in the past eleven years alone over 24,358 people have been saved. To wear a Sikorsky rescue pin is seen as a badge of honor within the industry.[6]

Sikorsky himself believed that God had given him his original dream and had guided him throughout the process. Might our flood victim view a helicopter differently if Sikorsky was right and God was assisting him in dreaming of, designing, and producing a helicopter? Is it possible that years before the flood waters arrived, God had, via a dream, put in motion a rescue plan for this man watching treacherous waters rise?

I assert that God is intervening through common grace much more than we think. This concept may be new to you or your friends, so it'll be important to define and illustrate it. As we do so, perhaps God will become less hidden.

Defining Common Grace

Common grace has long been acknowledged by theologians. Consider the following definition:

Common grace is so-called because it is common to all mankind. Its benefits are experienced by the whole human race without discrimination between one person and another. . . . To common grace, then, we must thankfully attribute God's continuing care for his creation, as he provides for the needs of his creatures, restrains human society from becoming altogether intolerable and ungovernable, and makes it possible for mankind, though fallen, to live together in a generally orderly and cooperative manner, to show mutual forbearance, and to cultivate together the scientific, cultural, and economic pursuits of civilization.[7]

From this definition notice that God's continuing care for his creation involves key aspects. Through the creation of government, designed in part to enforce laws, and our moral conscience, which makes us aware of good and bad choices, he keeps us from being intolerable. If God didn't intervene and give us the idea of what a just government looks like or provide us an intuitive awareness of right and wrong, we'd live like animals. However, God isn't just a cosmic police officer. He in turn provides for our needs through scientific, cultural, and economic insights that cause us to flourish. Don't miss the key part of this definition—God doesn't merely help people who worship him. In addition to the laws of nature and the regularity of seasons by which we grow crops, he generously gives key insights, skills, and moments of inspiration to *both* those within and outside the Christian community.

Theologian Wayne Grudem makes an interesting point when he asserts that "we should recognize that unbelievers often receive more common grace than believers—they may be more skillful, harder working, more intelligent, more creative, or have more of the material benefits of this life to enjoy."[8] A key part of having engaging conversations about God with those outside the Christian community is showing how they exhibit the traits of common grace described in this book. Acknowledging the good and virtuous actions of our neighbors will allow a conversation to start positively and build from there. Many of the illustrations recorded here focus on how non-Christians have used God's gifts to better our collective lives.

Illustrating Common Grace

"Every good and perfect gift is from above," asserts the Scriptures, "coming down from the Father of the heavenly lights, who does not change like shifting shadows" (Jas 1:17). Notice a few things about this statement. First, these good gifts come down to everyone—the good, bad, and indifferent. Don't take this for granted. Second, if God were punitive, he could send good gifts to those who love him and give little to nothing to those who reject him! Last, James's reference to God as the Father of heavenly lights is to communicate that his gifts are as plentiful as the vast array of stars![9]

This idea of God's gifts coming down to us is certainly poetic, but it reminds us that God is aware of our struggles and responds by sending gifts. "They come from above," notes commentator Paul Cedar, "because that is James' concept of where God is. Literally, they come from God."[10] James's language reminds me of a vivid example in the widely popular young adult series The Hunger Games. Suzanne Collins's postapocalyptic world resonates with readers of all ages and has been translated into twenty-six languages. In this disturbing world, children fight for their lives but can also find they are the unexpected recipients of timely gifts.

HUNGER GAMES AND PARACHUTES OF ASSISTANCE

In a postapocalyptic future the leaders of the nation of Panem punish dissenters and discourage rebellion by forcing each of the twelve districts to select a boy and girl from their own to compete in the Hunger Games. The entire nation watches as children fight to the death until a sole winner arises and is granted immunity. Katniss Everdeen and Peeta Mellark are selected to fight on behalf of District 12. Soon after the game begins Peeta is severely injured and hiding in a cave. While looking for food, Katniss sees a canister attached to a parachute floating to the ground. Inside the canister is a healing balm meant to save Peeta's life. Where did the canister come from? A unique part of the Hunger Games is that benefactors watching in elaborate viewing rooms can, if so moved, send the fighters precious gifts (medicine, food, a compass). These gifts often prove to be the difference between life and death!

The same is true with God. As he watches a world in rebellion, he graciously sends to the warring world gifts such as medical discoveries (penicillin, antibiotics, X-ray machines), survival tools (bows and arrows to hunt, traps for catching animals, staffs to assist walking), the sense of morality (being able to distinguish between justice and injustice), ideas of what a virtuous government looks like (laws that punish evil and reward good), artistic expressions that help us conceive of the good life (poetry, music, art, live presentations), and so on. Instead of idly standing by and watching us suffer, he—like the benefactors in the Hunger Games—strategically sends gifts to us that make a sinful world more bearable.

GOING DEEPER

What are we to make of the insight, compassion, or morality of an unbeliever? For theologians like Richard Mouw the doctrine of common grace affirms human depravity while it also "honors the insights into the human predicament and the glimpses of grace and reconciliation we find in the best non-Christian philosophy, art, and political theory."[11] In the Sermon on the Mount we see Jesus holding this tension when he recognizes that non-Christian parents can still give good gifts to their children (Mt 7:11). Paul picks up this theme in Romans where he states that pagans—via their God-given conscience—feel affirmation for doing good and guilt for doing evil (Rom 2:15). This inner conviction explains why so many secular books on activism describe a "helper's high" that comes from civic action.

As God watches a rebellious world, he's moved by compassion to intervene. But how? While the gifts he sends don't come with parachutes, they often come through ideas or discoveries. Have you ever wondered where inventions come from? Volumes have been written about the creative process. Most experience an "aha moment" when everything comes together. This breakthrough often occurs when a person has been fixating on a problem or issue and has grown increasingly frustrated. And when they take a break, the magic occurs. Many inventors report that while doing something unrelated a connection is made between seemingly unrelated objects or situations.

Creative consultant Roger von Oech describes this aha moment as *a whack on the side of the head.*

HOW DO YOU HEAR A HUMAN HEARTBEAT?

In the early 1800s physicians were growing increasingly frustrated while trying to understand the complexities of the human heart. At the time, doctors simply placed their ear to a patient's chest to listen for irregularities. French physician René Laennec found this method ineffective when trying to listen to the irregular heartbeat of a patient who was overweight. There must be a better way! Walking to work one day he observed some boys playing with a long section of pipe. One boy would whisper at the end of the pipe and the other would listen from the other end and guess what was being said. From observing the reaction of the boys, Laennec could tell that most of the time they were spot-on. Laennec had an aha moment: *Couldn't I do the same while trying to listen to a patient's heart?* It was then that the modern stethoscope was born. Laennec started with a rolled-up newspaper and moved on to different forms of wooden shafts. In the early 1900s the stethoscope was refined to include ear tips, ear tubes, tubing, headset, stem, chest piece, diaphragm, and bell. However, Laennec's original idea was the genesis, and today we can't imagine a doctor's visit without it.

Where does this whack on the side of the head come from? If James is right and every good gift comes from above, then could it be that God has been working—in cooperation with us—to supply strategic whacks on the side of our head? Whenever I make this assertion, people often respond, "How could you ever know that?" Couldn't it just be a creative person coming up with a unique solution to a problem? I readily admit that I can't prove God is nudging a person to make a discovery. But there are some interesting clues. What if you learned that at the same time Laennec was conceiving of a stethoscope, doctors across the world were thinking along the same lines, motivated by similar aha moments? With little interaction the same crude medical invention was being discovered. *Well, that would be interesting but not surprising since they could send letters or use the telegraph*, you may be thinking. You are correct. Designs for the telegraph were being created by Samuel Morse in the 1830s, and sending a transatlantic letter would take months but could get there eventually.

However, what if there was a time when no global communication was possible but similar aha moments were occurring in diverse locations?

If you were to Google "ancient inventions" you would find lists not only identifying key inventions or discoveries but a ranking of which was the *most* important. While the rankings would differ slightly in order of priority, there is a remarkable agreement of what makes the list. For fun, what would you list as the top early inventions that changed human history? Compare your list with the experts.

Ancient Inventions That Changed the World

Tools: Whether made of stone or bones of animals, these crude instruments helped to dig or butcher animals.

Fire: How do you stay warm on bitterly cold nights, cook meat, or defend yourself from animal or human predators?

Art: From colored perforated beads to cave paintings to decorated seashells, our ancestors felt the need to express themselves.

Shoes: We need to not only protect feet but travel greater distances across rough or mountainous terrain.

Wheels: Wheeled transportation not only allowed mobility but was the start of widespread trade among different groups.

While looking at this list, notice a few important details. First, artifacts of these ancient inventions are found across civilizations. For example, historians quibble about who first could control fire—it's usually a tie between Africa and the Middle East—but they note that all cultures eventually did control fire.[12] Second and more importantly, while these discoveries were happening, there was no communication between cultures. None. Consider what an ancient Zoom conference might have sounded like between ancient cultures.

GROUP 1   What are you all working on this week? Anything useful?

GROUP 2   Yes! Do your feet ever hurt?

GROUP 1   Always! Stepping on rocks or thorns is really getting old!

GROUP 2   You gotta try something called a *shoe*!

GROUP 1   Your picture froze for a second. A what?

GROUP 2   *S-h-o-e*—you wear it on the bottom of your feet, and it really works! I'll send some rough sketches.

GROUP 3   Well, we're working on something called *fire*!

Unlike at the time of Laennec's stethoscope, when Morse code and transatlantic travel were also emerging, there was no chance ancient cultures—divided by oceans—were trading ideas. Yet each was roughly receiving the same whack on the side of the head. Is it possible these aha moments were coming from God?

Appealing to common grace does not offer a definitive argument for God's existence or an undisputable sign of divine action. Rather, it's meant to do several things. First, it helps the Christian community understand how a faithful God is acting daily to meet the needs of a fallen world. Common grace isn't the only way God acts, but it is a powerful sign he's committed to humanity as a whole. Second, examples or illustrations of common grace can pique the interest of those outside the Christian community to ask more questions about God and evidence for his reality.[13]

If we start to see evidence of God's compassion and activity in human inventions and discoveries, then the objection "Where is God?" will perhaps wane. This is the conclusion Pascal came to when he wrote that for him the hiddenness of God diminished when he realized that everything bore the stamp of the divine.[14]

GOING DEEPER

The strategy I and others have adopted is taken from Christian thinker and author C. S. Lewis. Lewis observes that diverse ancient civilizations exhibited roughly the same moral intuition. Each of these diverse cultures "had an idea that they ought to behave in a certain way."[15] Lewis's point is that if you compared the moral teachings of ancient Egyptians, Hindus, Chinese, Greeks, and Babylonians you'd see a remarkable similarity, not a

radical difference. Remember, these ancient cultures
had no contact with each other but still came up with
similar moral codes. So, what's a reasonable explanation? Lewis argues that God collectively moved human
hearts to discover a universal moral code. In the appen-
dix of his classic book *The Abolition of Man*, he offers a
stunning chart that lays out the eerie similarities between diverse cultures.[16] The same is true in arguing for
God's common grace—how do you explain similar
inventions popping up across diverse civilizations that
had no contact with each other? It seems a good idea is
hard to keep down.

Objections

The concept of common grace I've been presenting evokes an
interesting response from different camps. Christians respond
that the view of God I'm presenting can be a little disappointing.
"You seem to be presenting a God who is limited to stethoscopes
and the occasional creative invention. I want God to be bigger
than that." Remember, no single doctrine ever stands by itself.
The doctrine of common grace must be supplemented with
other doctrines such as God's omnipotence or unlimited power.
God speaks through the prophet Jeremiah and boldly proclaims,
"I am the LORD, the God of all mankind. Is anything too hard
for me?" (Jer 32:27). In a world of turmoil we take great comfort
in Jeremiah's proclamation. Yet we must resist the urge to expect
God to always wield his power in dramatic ways. For example,
in the United States over thirty-five million people suffer from
migraine headaches.[17] Lucky me, I'm one of them. Can God

heal me from my migraines? The prophet Jeremiah would un-equivocally respond in the affirmative. In fact, I know of a person who—after intense prayer—had their migraines sud-denly cease. I too have petitioned God and solicited the prayers of others. Yet my migraines persist. I manage due to the guidance of a neurologist and migraine medication.

Am I disappointed in not being outright healed? Sometimes a little; often a lot. Like the man on the roof of a house sur-rounded by flood waters, I want God to miraculously intervene. Over time I've grown more open to the idea that being rescued via a helicopter or boat *is* God acting. When hungry, do people care if food comes through Jesus multiplying loaves (Mt 14:19-21) or through the ancient church sharing food with the needy (Jas 2:15-16)? Subsequently, I now view my migraine medication as a form of common grace and am thankful to God for it.

Those in the non-Christian camp can sometimes feel slighted by the notion human advancement is ultimately attributed to God's grace. Not everyone is ready to give God all or even some of the credit. When Covid-19 infection numbers and death rates finally dropped in New York during the summer of 2020, a be-leaguered Governor Andrew Cuomo shocked people with his candidness: "The number is down because we brought the number down. God did not do that. Faith did not do that. Destiny did not do that. A lot of pain and suffering did that. . . . That's how it works."[18] You may get a similar reaction from your friend: "So, it's all God? It's him whacking us on the side of the head while we twiddle our thumbs?"

Not at all. Even a cursory reading of the Bible informs us that God wants to work in partnership with his human creation. In the creation mandate Adam and Eve are given the responsibility to govern the earth. Couldn't God just do it himself? Yes, but why then create human partners? Adam and Eve, in conjunction with God, would use their creativity—agriculture, tool making, organizing communities, shepherding animals—to manage our diverse world. This partnership continues in a fallen world where the armies of Israel defend themselves using weapons (tools) and military strategies (problem solving) rather than merely leaning on divine intervention. This carries into the New Testament where God boldly states that true religion is caring for the marginalized (Jas 1:27) and partners with the church to organize and distribute food and clothing (Acts 6:1-7). James shocks a young church when he informs them they do not have because they did not consult with God (Jas 4:2). The sense you get from biblical writers is that God wants to mentor us rather than doing it all himself.

THE ROLE OF A MENTOR

Denzel Washington is arguably the best actor of his generation, having garnered two Golden Globe Awards, one Tony Award, and two Academy Awards: one for acting in the Civil War drama *Glory* (1989) and the other for portraying a rogue narcotics detective in *Training Day* (2001). In addition, he's tackled larger-than-life characters like controversial activist Malcolm X and wrongly accused boxer Rubin "Hurricane" Carter. What's the secret of his success? Washington candidly states, "I don't care what you do for a living—if you do it well I'm sure there was someone cheering you on or showing the way. A mentor."[19] Denzel has no issue with the idea that his growth or success as an actor was partially dependent on one key factor—a mentor.

Does having a mentor somehow cheapen or diminish Denzel's accomplishments? Is it the mentor who does everything while Washington sits idly by? No. The mentor helped occasionally by "showing the way" and offering encouragement to an aspiring actor. The same is true with God and us. As collective humanity faces challenges and hardships, God partners with us by showing the way when we are stuck and providing encouragement to reach biblical ideals he's placed in the human heart (Rom 2:15). He does this willingly and compassionately for a world that for the most part has rejected him. "You are a gracious and compassionate God," concludes the prophet Jonah, "slow to anger and abounding in love" (Jon 4:2).

Becoming aware of God's action in the world will require a change in what C. S. Lewis called the "seeing eye." When asked about a Russian astronaut's bold claim that he did not see God in outer space, Lewis responded: "To some, God is discoverable everywhere; to others, nowhere. Those who do not find Him on earth are unlikely to find Him in space. But send a saint up in a spaceship and he'll find God in space as he found God on earth. Much depends on the seeing eye."[20] Interestingly, Lewis argues that we often miss God due to our inattention. "One obstacle is inattention. One could simply hear the roar and not the roaring of the wind. And ignore the smell of Deity that hangs about it."[21] In the following chapters we'll seek to expand the "seeing eye" of our skeptical friends and neighbors by helping them focus on God's activity in daily life.

Conclusion

God didn't merely provide ancient civilizations with common grace resulting in key discoveries such as fire, tools, and the wheel. He continues to mentor—showing us the way—as we face modern challenges.

By his own account, Sam Sheridan is a free spirit who spent time as a merchant marine, amateur mixed martial arts fighter, EMS worker, and construction foreman in Antarctica. He wasn't prepared, however, for his greatest challenge—being a dad. "Here's the bittersweet truth of having a child: it entails the loss of a kind of narcissism, the end of your own childhood."[22] Suddenly, he took seriously all the apocalyptic stories he devoured as a single. What if my family encountered a cataclysmic event? What would I need to know to protect them in a suddenly chaotic and dangerous world? The result is his book *The Disaster Diaries* in which he imagines threats—loss of clean water, a child with a broken bone, coping with PTSD, cars that no longer start, hand-to-hand combat with strangers—and sought experts in each field. From wilderness survivalists he learned to trap wild game, build an igloo, and determine which flowers could heal or kill him. A leading psychologist gave him a crash course on stress inoculation and how to keep his loved ones from spiraling into depression. He spent weeks with a Buddhist monk learning to be mindful in extreme situations. A martial arts expert gave him strategies in how to stop bad people in their tracks, while merely subduing a person engulfed in raw fear.

In the end he found that his greatest resource was the space "between my own ears." By consulting experts, gathering knowledge, and learning new skills, he gradually felt more equipped. "I've broadened and deepened my understanding of the world, almost immeasurably."[23] In the following chapters we'll join Sheridan by exploring the world around us. A world saturated with common grace and filled with strategic gifts meant to protect and enlighten us. And we'll learn to explain and illustrate those gifts to a skeptical world.

Further Reading

Abraham Kuyper, *Common Grace: God's Gift for a Fallen World*, vol. 1 (Bellingham, WA: Lexham, 2015).

Richard Mouw, *All That God Cares About: Common Grace and Divine Delight* (Ada, MI: Brazos, 2020).

CHAPTER TWO

God the Scientist

HEALING GRACE IN A SICK WORLD

Imagine a world without science.

Gone is an astronaut standing on the lunar surface holding
an American flag. A medicine cabinet filled with band-aids, aspirin, toothpaste, eye drops, and antibacterial wipes is empty. A
desk once covered with a laptop computer, smart phone, multicolor spreadsheets, and cup of coffee is now cleared and covered
in dust. "Let's *not* imagine a world without science" concludes
the forty-eight-second commercial. Still shaken by the idea of
life without a cell phone or coffee, we agree!

Gladly, we don't need to imagine such a world. When God
gave Adam and Eve the creation mandate (Gen 1:28; 2:15), he
ushered in the age of science. Taken from the Latin word *scientia*, science simply means "knowledge." Religion writer
Rebecca McLaughlin posits that the "God who made the universe must have scientific knowledge as far surpassing ours as a
street lamp is surpassed by the sun!"[1] Being made in God's
image includes a natural inclination toward scientific inquiry.

To manage creation—name animals, grow crops, mine for minerals, feed and care for livestock, work in concert with seasons—the first humans had to study creation. Far from religion being at odds with science, scientific inquiry is central to fulfilling God's purpose for us. If science was important for the first human couple inhabiting paradise, imagine how essential it is for us living in a fallen world. A world that shuns God is not a safe place. Without scientific knowledge, life on this planet would be impossible. Our goal as Christian communicators is to help our skeptical friends understand both the dangers of our world and how God has graciously provided scientific knowledge to meet these threats.

GOING DEEPER

Scientific knowledge would be useless if God didn't give us another key component of common grace—our rational capacity to observe and make sense of the world around us. If not for our ability to investigate, conduct experiments, and note patterns, we might never comprehend the speed of light, the presence of germs, the stability of physical laws, or the workings of the human body. God not only gave us science but also the ability to be students of nature—human scientists.

Science and Mars

To make the necessity of science even more pronounced, let's temporarily shift our focus from our planet to one that has long captured our imagination—Mars. Currently, NASA has a goal

of sending astronauts to the Red Planet in 2033. What would be
the challenges when they arrive, and how could science help?

The biggest challenge will be to simply stay alive in an atmosphere that is one hundred times thinner than Earth's. Why is
that such a big deal? The atmosphere we breathe in every day is
made up of 78 percent nitrogen and 21 percent oxygen with
trace amounts of carbon dioxide. Mars's atmosphere is a
whopping 95 percent carbon dioxide! Add to this freezing temperatures (at night minus 65 degrees Fahrenheit) and radiation
levels that would cause your blood to boil. Welcome to Mars—
a seemingly inhospitable world! Then why is NASA so set
on getting to Mars in 2033? Because science is up for
the challenge.

The blockbuster movie *The Martian* (2015) asks a provocative
question: If abandoned on Mars, how long could a person
survive? Based on the facts we've just considered, the answer
seems obvious—not very long. The Golden Globe–nominated
film for best picture, directed by Ridley Scott, challenges
that assumption.

SCIENCE TO THE RESCUE

In 2035 the fictional crew of *Ares III* has to abandon their
mission to Mars when they encounter a massive life-
threatening dust storm. As evacuation commences the
captain wrongly assumes that one of their crew, Mark
Watney (played by Matt Damon), has died in the dust
storm. As *Ares III* leaves Mars's atmosphere, we learn that
Watney was only rendered unconscious. He wakes up
alone and frightened, but not hopeless. As one of the
mission's scientists, he returns to the surface habitat and

goes to work. After attending to his wounds, he sets out to create a garden utilizing Martian soil and human waste. He plants unused potatoes—intended for a Mars Thanksgiving celebration—and nurtures them with water strained from leftover rocket fuel. Without the space rocket's communications links, Watney devises a clever system of communication to get NASA's attention, "I'm alive!" You'll have to watch the rest of the movie to see how it ends. But a dangerous situation is lessened through scientific ingenuity.

The more we think about Mark Watney's struggle to survive on Mars, the more it becomes obvious that life on Earth—while not perfect—is much better suited for us. Though not as dangerous as Mars, our planet offers serious challenges of its own. Take a minute and think of some of the potential or current threats we are facing (e.g., pandemics, cancer, poverty, global warming). As you consider these threats, you may begin to wonder why God hasn't done more to stop them. Certainly, he has the power to stop global warming or cancer! Yet they remain. Why? In my conversations with others, this question seems to pop up over and over. How might we answer?

Science and Earth

Our world is a mess because we, frankly, are a spiritual mess. Our human rebellion not only spiritually separated us from God (Is 53:6) but also deeply affected life on our planet. "The creation was subjected to frustration," asserts the apostle Paul (Rom 8:20). Our English word *frustration* comes from the Greek word *mataiotēs*, which primarily means futility. The planet is locked into a futile cycle that includes not only birth, growth,

and production but also decline, decay, disease, and ultimately
death. This cycle of birth, growth, decay, and death greatly
grieves God. In a shocking passage God declares that after
watching us and his creation fall into disarray, his heart was
"deeply troubled" (Gen 6:6). In short, the world is not as God
desires. Rather than washing his hands of us, he intervenes by
imparting knowledge via science.

How does science help us in a world immersed in futility?

GOING DEEPER

Paul's claim the world has been subjected to frustration
(*mataiotēs*) also carries with it the reality of spiritual
battle and an adversary who wants to distort God's
common grace. Life on our planet is made difficult by an
adversary who wants to take what is good (creation)
and warp it. Thus, the very weather that nourishes crops
can also turn into tornadoes or hurricanes. Fire can be
used as heat on cold nights or as a devastating weapon
(flamethrowers, scorched-earth tactics). Surely, to be
biblical is to understand the world currently lies in the
hand of the evil one (1 Jn 5:19), and his sinister work is at
play. However, not all is lost. Paul offers hope when he
states that while the earth was subjected to futility, it
was done so with liberation in mind (Rom 8:20). For sure,
Paul is referencing the ultimate redemption of humanity
and our planet powerfully described in Revelation 20.
However, applying an inaugurated eschatology motif
(already–not yet), the earth is partially liberated every
time humans use science to understand the original
intent of creation, use knowledge to heal our planet

(conservation, climate control, ecology), and act as
creation caretakers.

Our Amazing Immune System

In many ways we need to navigate the same challenges that the
fictitious Watney faced on the unforgiving red dust of Mars:
helping our bodies heal from injury, producing clean food and
water, and traveling long distances through difficult terrain.
Through his common grace God has provided scientific
knowledge and technology to help. For the sake of time let's
focus on one key aspect of science—understanding how our
bodies work and how to keep them functioning properly.

To survive in a fallen world filled with disease and sickness,
God has provided us protection—the human body. God has also
given us knowledge (science) that has led to crucial medicinal
drugs and interventions. But let's start with our greatest natural
defense—our immune system.

In his book *A Little History of Science*, medical historian
William Bynum asserts that from the beginning doctors have understood that their job was to assist the natural healing process of
the human body. "Doctors sometimes joke among themselves that
if they treat a disease it will be gone in a week, but if they don't it
will take seven days."[2] Scientists and doctors understand something we often take for granted—our amazing *immune system*.

Our immune system protects our body against disease or
foreign bodies that may damage us. Our system first identifies
and then attacks viruses, bacteria, or parasites.

THANK GOD FOR FEVERS

You're sick! You know you are because you are running a fever. Before you reach for meds to lower it, understand a fever is a key weapon in your immune system's arsenal. Right now, there are millions of white blood cells, including T cells, flowing through your body looking for harmful bacteria or viruses. While you are unaware of them, they quietly flow along the bloodstream looking for a potential threat. Like a roving sentry, these cells are always on alert. When a threat is detected, the body causes a fever that kicks these T cells into high gear! As our temperatures rise, our blood moves more quickly pushing T cells to the site of the threat, and the battle is on. Immediately lowering a temperature is like putting speed bumps in the path of these crucial cells. After we recover and regain our health, it's easy to forget a particular bout with a virus. Not so for T cells. Research shows that T cells remember threatening pathogens long after they're gone and in essence create a "reference library of past battles."[3]

Imagine life without an immune system or fast-acting T cells: Our atmosphere—filled with germs—would be deadly. Going outside for a walk or stepping out your front door at night to look at the stars could be fatal. Tragically, for David Vetter this nightmare scenario became reality.

BOY IN THE BUBBLE

Born September 21, 1971, David spent only seconds in his mother's arms before being rushed into a plastic isolation tube. Tests had predetermined he would be born with severe combined immunodeficiency (SCID), a rare disease that short-circuits an entire immune system. Any exposure to germs or disease would be fatal. NASA scientists helped doctors at Texas Children's Hospital in Houston create a large plastic bubble to keep out all threats, and David was soon dubbed by the press as the boy in the bubble. Water, food, diapers, and clothes had to be carefully sterilized before entering the bubble. Each item was subjected to heat at 140 degrees Fahrenheit and then aerated for seven days and triple-checked for pathogens. David was fed, washed, and held by parents and nurses via plastic sleeves meticulously sealed off from threats. Gradually, David learned of an outside world filled with other children, playgrounds, schools, and most importantly movie theaters. He wanted to participate. Again, NASA jumped into action and designed a space suit that David could wear so he could go outside for carefully orchestrated outings. Getting into the suit entailed a fifty-two-step process. It worked. David spent his eleventh birthday in his parent's backyard looking up at stars, followed by going to a private showing of *Return of the Jedi* at a local theater. It was the best day of his life.

Sadly, David would die one year later after a failed bone-marrow treatment. Today, kids with SCID live fairly normal lives due to David donating his blood cells for research. His memory lives on through the David Center at Texas Children's Hospital, where research into our immune system continues.[4] Without our God-given immune system, we'd all have to live like David in plastic bubbles.

GOING DEEPER

What does our immune system tell us about God's relation to social justice and caring for the marginalized? According to the World Health Organization (WHO) and the World Bank, more than half of the world goes without basic health services (just under four billion people).[5] Many in the world have to make the tragic choice of whether to spend money on food or health care. The only protection against a world of disease and sickness for these individuals is their immune system. Not only is God aware of this tragedy, but he also provided basic health protection to all regardless of socioeconomic status! As David's story shows, our immune systems can be compromised or even severely damaged. However, without our immunes systems, we all would have to live in completely sterilized contexts.

While the effect of living in a fallen world is seen in the crippling of David's God-given immune system, God's common grace is evident in NASA scientists' life-saving ingenuity and advances in our understanding of how to treat challenges to our immune system. While few people will face something as severe as SCID, there are times when our immune system needs help. God is aware of these complications and partners with scientists and doctors to find ways to augment our first line of defense.

If you've ever had a nasty sinus infection, strep throat, bronchitis, or pneumonia, then you know there are times when your immune system needs assistance! Antibiotics are like elite commandos who take the fight directly to the bad bacteria in your system. In fact, if misused they can even hurt your immune system. How the first antibiotic was created mirrors Laennec's seemingly serendipitous discovery of the stethoscope and again opens the door for signs of divine prodding.

PRAISE FOR SLOPPY LAB TECHS

Alexander Fleming was a lab technician at St. Mary's Hospital in London in the 1920s. While dedicated, he had a reputation as being slightly careless in cleaning the lab. When he returned from a two-week vacation, he was irritated to find mold partly growing on a petri dish. As he went to clean it, he noticed that the mold prevented the bacteria (staphylococcus) on parts of the dish from growing. He identified the mold as coming from *penicillium* and did some more tests. While he thought it promising, he moved on to other projects. Thankfully, he wrote up his observations in a paper that was published and read by a handful of bacteriologists, but soon it was forgotten. A decade later, during the Second World War, scientist Howard Florey was asked by the British government to look for ways to keep soldiers from infectious diseases common to the bloody battlefields of Europe. After reading hundreds of obscure research papers, he stumbled upon Fleming's paper and his mold observation. Soon, penicillin was being mass-produced in Britain and the United States, saving not only soldiers but anyone facing harmful bacteria.

Years later Fleming would marvel that one mold-covered petri dish would lead to the first antibiotic. "One sometimes finds what one is not looking for," quipped Fleming. "I certainly didn't plan to revolutionize all medicine by discovering the world's first antibiotic, or bacteria killer. But I guess that was exactly what I did."[6] While historian William Bynum calls the discovery of penicillin a "lucky chance," is it possible that something else was at work?[7] Is it *possible* that God, serving as a mentor to scientists, gave Fleming a nudge to notice the bacteria-killing mold and helped Florey uncover an obscure research paper? While not definitive, it is at least possible. Remember, as a Christian communicator our goal is to foster curiosity in our friends to have more conversations about evidence for God's existence.

Objection: Evolution and Our Immune System

Sometimes while making the argument that our immune system and the antibiotics that strengthen it are equally God-given, I've received some pushback. While speaking on a college campus, one student asked a thoughtful question, "While you say God is responsible for our immune system, I say it's a product of evolution. Over time we simply evolved to face a harsh environment filled with dangerous bacteria and disease. Doesn't that make more sense?"

The objection of evolution is a serious one and will be revisited in upcoming chapters. For now, two responses may be helpful. First, for certain people of faith, evolution is not a dealbreaker. While a small group, there are those within Christianity who believe the evolution process was not entirely random but, rather, was guided by God, resulting in the gradual creation of humankind. This perspective includes influential voices from Christian scientists, apologists, philosophers, and political theorists. Conversely, their view is opposed by an equally impressive group of Christian scholars.[8] However, it's important to affirm that the rejection of evolution is *not* a necessary prerequisite to becoming a Jesus follower. Pastor and author Tim Keller offers sound advice for those checking out religion but are persuaded by evidence for evolution: "Since Christian believers occupy different positions on both the meanings of Genesis 1 and on the nature of evolution, those who are considering Christianity as a whole should not allow themselves to be distracted by this intramural debate."[9]

Second, for those of us who are leery of embracing any version of unguided macroevolution, it may be good to offer reasons and an illustration or two for your reluctance. What might fuel this opposition to evolution? It's one thing for the college student to argue that our immune systems evolved and spread throughout humanity, but *how* does this happen practically? In a Christian worldview God is the one who crafted our immune system and wired it into humanity just like an expert craftsperson weaves a complex basket (Ps 139:13). Yet, via evolution, how do positive or advantageous genetic traits—like an immune system—get passed on from person to person or community to community? Casey Luskin, a cofounder of the Intelligent Design and Evolution Awareness Center, posits that proponents of evolution "often assume that once mutations produce a functionally advantageous trait, it will easily spread (become 'fixed') throughout a population by natural selection." Makes sense, doesn't it? If an immune system is advantageous to our survival, then it will spread everywhere, ensuring our survival. Not so fast, suggests Luskin. A harsh reality for evolutionists is the fact that "random forces or events can prevent a trait from spreading through a population, even when it provides an advantage."[10] Luskin is referring to something called the *bottleneck effect*. To make sense, I've found the following helpful illustration.

A DIVERSE MARBLE COLLECTION

A boy loves marbles. Whenever asked what he wants as a gift, it's *always* marbles. Therefore, birthdays, Christmases, and special events all yield the same present—marbles. The boy longs for a diverse marble collection that contains every color available. Whenever they are shopping, family members, friends, and relatives pick up a pack of marbles and give it to him. Years go by and soon the boy is close to having all the colors and takes his jar of marbles to school to show off. As he leaves the bus, he stumbles and drops his jar! Most of the marbles fall into a storm drain never to be recovered! Heartbroken, he's left with a random collection of marbles consisting of eight red marbles and one blue. His dream of a diverse collection is gone.

What does this have to do with evolution and our immune system? Imagine the marbles in the bottle represent a population with genetic diversity, including some who—purely by chance—are evolving the necessary components of our immune system. Over time through breeding, genes (including an immune system) will be passed on to the entire population. Maybe, maybe not. Two aspects of the marble illustration work against evolution providing our immune system.

First, evolutionists want to suggest that those purchasing marbles are organized and guided by a common goal—providing the boy with a diverse marble collection. So, before they buy marbles, the boy's relatives and friends check in with each other to make sure they are picking up different marbles. "Hey, no more black marbles; we need more reds and blues." However, Luskin's central critique of naturalistic evolution is that it's *un*guided and cannot anticipate the needs of an organism. Thus, the boy's gift-givers *never* check with each other and simply buy whatever pack of marbles they happen to see in a store. If the boy's marble collection is diverse, it's just the luck of the draw. And if friends are randomly purchasing marbles, a diverse collection may never happen! The same is true of our immune system—if evolution is unguided, there is no guarantee we'll develop what we need to fend off disease.

Second, dropping the jar represents a catastrophic bottleneck event such as attacks from other communities or animals, fire, disease, or other natural disasters that result in the majority of the population being killed off. The few marbles that didn't go down the drain—by chance—survive. But what if the marbles left are mostly one color? The boy's hopes of a diverse collection are gone. A bottleneck event presents the same challenge to evolution creating our immune system. After a catastrophic event, what if no one with an evolving immune system made it? Tragically, the survivors who remain will have to do without an immune system until they come in contact with individuals from other communities and hope that they can develop one before another bottleneck event sets them back again. Seems odd that our survival seems to be a mere matter of genetic chance.[11]

If talk of marbles and bottlenecks gets confusing, consider this real-life example.

SAVE THE SEALS

Years ago elephant seals were mercilessly hunted for oil-rich blubber. Only through intervention from the US government were the seals able to start to recover. Once down to one hundred seals, the population is now over thirty thousand. The killing of the seals was a bottleneck event dramatically decreasing the seal population and genetic diversity. Only under the protection of the US government were seals allowed to breed. Interestingly, seal colonies consist of one dominant male seal that can impregnate over one hundred females. Thus, some seal populations can be traced back to one male. While scientists are encouraged by the growth in the seal population, they fear the lack of genetic diversity could result in the entire population being wiped out by a single pathogen or disease. The genetic diversity and immunity to disease were greatly compromised by a bottleneck event (mass hunting). It may take centuries for the seal community to gain genetic diversity and immunity. In the meantime, they are at great risk.

Luskin is not the only one who is skeptical that natural selection can effectively—and quickly—give us what we need to survive. In fact, he points out that more than a thousand scientists with PhDs have signed a statement agreeing they are "skeptical of claims for the ability of random mutation and natural selection to account for the complexity of life."[12]

Objection: Science Cancels Faith

While the objection of evolution is very specific, I've regularly encountered questions spurred on by a prevailing assumption.

"I thought the whole point of science is that it shows religion to be obsolete? I've always thought the two were at war with each other?" This common misperception seems to be rooted in the idea that you can be either a person of faith or a person of science—but not both! This assumption is powerfully articulated by atheist philosopher Alex Rosenberg, who boldly asserts that atheism is "a demanding, rigorous, breathtaking grip on reality, one that has been vindicated beyond reasonable doubt. It's called science."[13]

How should you respond?

In a twenty-four-hour news cycle made accessible via smartphones, laptop computers, television, or old-fashioned print media, we are bombarded with provocative claims. How can we know which claims are true? In the age of the internet, fact-checking has become a crucial skill. Do facts support the idea that religion has no place in the world of science?

When asked if God exists, 95 percent of Americans state they believe in some type of deity or higher power. Specifically, eight in ten Americans say they believe in God. How would scientists respond to the same question? Based on Rosenberg's claim that atheism is vindicated by science, the numbers must be low, or even nonexistent. Right? Surprisingly, over half of scientists (51 percent) in America hold a belief in a higher power or some type of deity, while 33 percent say they believe in God.[14] Do you find these statistics surprising? Add to these stats that some of the *who's who* of science have held to a firm belief in God.

If you made a list of the *most* significant movers and shakers of history, who would make it? Historian Michael Hart takes up this challenge and gives us a thought-provoking list of the one hundred most influential people ranked in order. In his introduction he states that the two most powerful forces in history have been science and religion. Thus, the top two spots on his list are persons representing each.[15] Muhammad—the founder of Islam—is selected by Hart to represent religion and snags the coveted top spot due to his influence on diverse realms such as religion, politics, and the military. Who does Hart pick to represent science and assume the second slot? Noted scientists such as Einstein, Pasteur, Galileo, Aristotle, or Darwin are all great choices and are firmly entrenched in the top twenty. But Hart selects Sir Isaac Newton.

Most likely, the only thing most people have heard about Newton is that an apple supposedly fell on his head and he discovered gravity. Yes, Newton was among the first to postulate gravity, but there's much more!

LOST LETTERS OF NEWTON

During his lifetime (1643–1727) Newton is not only credited with the theory of gravity (sorry, the apple falling on his head never happened) but also laying the groundwork for modern physics, conceptualizing calculus, and a breakthrough in optics that led to the reflecting telescope. Upon Newton's death the French philosopher Voltaire commented, "He was buried like a king who had done well by his subjects."[16] It's no wonder Newton is to this day revered as one of the finest scientists to ever live. He's also one of the most studied scholars in history. That's why in 1936 when his letters were auctioned, the world was shocked to learn that science wasn't Newton's first love. Rather, theology was what *most* captured Newton's attention. It's been speculated that Newton wrote over one million words ruminating about God, miracles, prophecy, and prayer. In his letters Newton describes weeks when science was cast aside in order to study the Bible uninterrupted. One researcher concluded that Newton saw science as a religious duty where a "knowledge of God's power and wisdom could be inferred from the intelligence seemingly displayed in the designs of nature."[17] Apparently, Newton—selected by Hart to represent all of science—had no problem being a person of science and faith!

GOING DEEPER

What was the "intelligence" Newton observed in the designs of nature? Unlike the harsh climate of Mars, it seems Earth's environment is fine-tuned for us. If the variables of our planet were altered even a little, life would be impossible. In other words, a lot had to come together just right so we could exist on this planet. Consider the following:

The moon. The Earth has a slight tilt and teeters like a top as it spins, which can cause drastic shifts in climate over the course of thousands of years. But because of the moon's stabilizing effect on our orbit, our climate is steadier.

Magnetic field. Our planet is blessed with a strong, stable magnetic field, which staves off the cosmic rays and solar flares that would otherwise fry the planet now and then.

Stable rotation. There's no reason to think that a planet without a stable rotation would be completely inhabitable, but the regularity and frequency of day and

night on this planet go far to prevent extreme temperatures and encourage life.[18]

For scientists like Newton the idea that all these
factors just happened was not acceptable. It was more
reasonable—and scientific—to postulate a divine hand
guiding these factors. The personal care of the Creator
is noted by the prophet Isaiah, who states that God
"leads forth the starry host by number; He calls each
one by name. Because of His great power and mighty
strength, not one of them is missing" (Is 40:26 Berean
Study Bible).

What's interesting about discussing God and science is that
many people think Bible-believing experts like Newton are
relics and science has so advanced today that no accomplished
scientist would believe in the God of the Bible. Are there any
modern scientists who, like Newton, believe in God?

In her award-winning book *Confronting Christianity*,
Rebecca McLaughlin writes that she lives within walking distance of the hallowed halls of the Massachusetts Institute of
Technology (MIT). Their science program is considered the best
in the world and houses the most recognized scientists alive.
While there may be some professors at MIT who are open to the
possibility of an abstract higher power, what are the chances
there would be any Christian professors? McLaughlin produces
an impressive, yet partial, list:

- Ian Hutchinson (professor of nuclear science)
- Daniel Hastings (professor of astronautics)
- Jing Kong (professor of electrical engineering)

- Rosalind Picard (invented field of affective computing)
- Troy Van Voorhis (chemistry professor)
- Linda Griffith (biological and mechanical engineering professor)
- Dick Yue (professor of ocean engineering)
- Susan Hockfield (neuroscientist and former president of MIT)

McLaughlin concludes, "If science has disproved Christianity, no one has thought to notify them!"[19] For these accomplished scholars, science doesn't threaten faith but enriches it.

A Warning from Scientists About Science

In a world at odds with God, scientific gifts can easily turn into global threats. How can God get our attention to inform us that the world is perilously close to misusing science to threaten our very existence? The answer: a unique clock.

THE DOOMSDAY CLOCK

This ominous-sounding clock was not created by science-fiction writers or comic-book enthusiasts. Rather, it was created by atomic scientists who worked on the Manhattan Project and are now concerned that the atomic arms race they started could destroy our world. As the clock hands move closer to midnight, the scientists believe we are closer to global disaster. The hands move based on the current state of global nuclear threat, climate change, biosecurity, bioterrorism, and cyber warfare. Here are some of the dramatic moves toward midnight since the creation of the clock:

1947—7 minutes to midnight. First appearance of the clock registering fears of nuclear dangers between the United States and the Soviet Union.

1949—3 minutes to midnight. The Soviet Union tests its first atomic bomb.

1953—2 minutes to midnight. The United States creates the hydrogen bomb.

1984—3 minutes to midnight. US-Soviet relations reached their frostiest level in years.

2015—3 minutes to midnight. The clock registered deep concerns about unchecked climate change that could threaten global existence.

Where is the clock today?

2020—100 seconds (1 minute, 40 seconds) to midnight. The hands have never been closer to midnight due to increased nuclear tensions between the United States, Russia, and North Korea, augmented by an alarming rate of climate change.

The Scriptures state that there is a way that seems right to us—nuclear proliferation, gaining power through military force, using science to create advanced weaponry, stripping Earth's resources to fuel our industrial revolution—which may ultimately lead to death (Prov 14:12). Spurred on by God's concern, the Doomsday Clock demands our attention and advocates a different course of action—before it's too late.

Conclusion

As the Doomsday Clock reminds us, our world is filled with danger *and* wonder. The beauty of birth and life is challenged by disease, infection, and nuclear threat. Knowing the dangers that awaited us, God not only gave us an immune system but also supplied us with insight on how to strengthen our natural defenses. This knowledge was not limited to one economic class, elite medical professionals, or a block of countries that could hoard such life-saving information. "Science knows no country," asserts the father of germ theory, Louis Pasteur, "because knowledge belongs to humanity, and is the torch which illuminates the world."[20] Each step of our collective journey has been one of medical, technological, and scientific illumination. Where did this knowledge come from? Long before Pasteur discovered germs or refined the process of pasteurization, the ancient writers of the book of Proverbs asserted, "For the LORD gives wisdom; from his mouth come[s] knowledge" (Prov 2:6).

Further Reading

Greg Cootsona, *Mere Science and Christian Faith: Bridging the Divide with Emerging Adults* (Downers Grove, IL: InterVarsity Press, 2018).

J. P. Moreland, *Christianity and the Nature of Science: A Philosophical Investigation* (Grand Rapids, MI: Baker, 1989).

CHAPTER THREE

Art

GOD'S SPOTLIGHT ON THE HUMAN CONDITION

He sat dejected in an outdoor French café.

While taking a long pull on a cigarette, one of the greatest philosophers of the twentieth century was perplexed about how to get his thoughts out to the common people rushing past him. Jean-Paul Sartre had just completed a massive seven hundred-page book laying out his complex thoughts on existentialism, self-deception, free will, consciousness, and human perception. While *Being and Nothingness* was highly praised by literary critics and fellow philosophers, most found the page count daunting. It was a brilliant book largely ignored by fellow Parisians.

What to do?

Sartre's solution is one you've most likely read in high school or are at least familiar with, "Hell is other people." *No Exit* is Sartre's one-act play that focuses on the conversation between three characters who find themselves unexpectedly together in the afterlife. While covering the same topics of *Being and*

Nothingness, this modest sixty-page play can be read in one sitting and has been converted into a BBC broadcast, two feature films, a Broadway production, and operas in both New York and London. *No Exit* continues to influence serving as inspiration for the popular show *The Good Place* and for the series finale of *Seinfeld* where the main actors—much like Sartre's characters—unexpectedly find themselves sitting in a jail cell chatting. While *Being and Nothingness* is still revered by scholars, *No Exit* makes educators' must-read lists and continues to provoke our thinking. The power of art—be it a play, song, poetry, YouTube video, or hot new title from Netflix—is to expose us to truths about life in a fallen world.

Just as most people didn't make time for Sartre's seven-hundred-page tome, people today often fail to think deeply about the human condition. Art has a way of not only grabbing our attention but also showcasing both the good and bad. The arts are a powerful means of common grace that prompt us to reassess ourselves and our surroundings.

What's Art Supposed to Do?

Anyone who has taken a stroll to the modern art section of a gallery and looked at crudely drawn circles interconnecting in a seemingly haphazard way might ask, What's the purpose of this? That's a good question to ask your coworker after you discuss a new show on Amazon Prime or a novel you just can't put down. What's art supposed to do? The answer has been bandied about by critics, art professors, artists of diverse mediums, and every college freshman student forced to take an art appreciation class. I smile writing this as I think back to when my middle son, Jason, had to read a book on modern art for a required class in college.

As a budding law student, such abstract thinking was uninviting, to say the least. I'd hear him sighing as he turned pages. Finally, he exploded, shouting to me upstairs, "Dad, what's the big deal about art? Who needs it?" The answer to his question could fill volumes. Is the role of art to merely decorate blank walls, serve as a hobby for weekend painters, entertain, keep kids busy with crafts, or something more?

GOING DEEPER

Theologian Philip Ryken notes that God calls Bezalel to be the chief architect of the new tabernacle and reveals that he has filled him with "ability and intelligence, with knowledge and all craftsmanship, to devise artistic designs" (Ex 31:2-3). Apparently, God wasn't interested in a sterile place of worship but an artistic masterpiece. Is craftsmanship limited to a select few? No. Ryken notes that the cultural mandate (Gen 1:28) is not God's call merely to populate the world but to create civilizations, cities, and communities. "Culture is not *just* the arts, but the arts are certainly part of a culture's foundation. Art functions as both the soil for cultural growth and the fruit that it yields."[1] Thus, the knowledge of craftsmanship found in Bezalel seems to have been generally instilled in human artists worldwide. While cultural norms may vary, the one constant is that they equally express values through art.

How does God use our collective artistic inclination in a fallen world? Is art merely about aesthetic design, or can God use art to disturb us and question the status quo? While definitions of art are plentiful, in this chapter I'll adopt the perspective of *New York Times* art critic Michael Kustow, who states that every work of art is "a revolt in the name of fresh perspective."[2] The revolt happens when we move from being a child—who takes her surroundings for granted—to becoming an adult who begins to see their environment in a fresh way and wonder how they could be different. Kustow asserts that a key piece of artistic revolt "involves denial of an existing order." Thus, two crudely drawn circles seemingly intersecting with no purpose might challenge our desire for order and the assumption that all art should be easily interpreted. An exercise well worth our time.

God wants those same moments of reflection for each of us— to stop and see life in a fresh perspective. As creatures at odds with their Creator, it's easy to see our fractured way of life as normal. In the busyness of life, we simply fall in line with what our culture tells us to expect of family, love, politicians, career, money, and what counts as a good life. God has other ideas. Through art, he shakes us from this slumber and offers a fresh perspective on the good we should seek and the bad we should collectively shun. In part, art is a crucial expression of common grace God uses to grab our attention and force us to stop and ponder not only the world around us but *ourselves*.

GOING DEEPER

To a young church rooted in Ephesus, Paul prays that the "eyes of your heart" would be enlightened (Eph 1:18). In the ancient Greek language, the *heart* refers to all aspects of us—emotions, intellect, and volition. God isn't interested in people approaching spiritual truths merely on the cognitive level as a topic to be dispassionately studied. Rather, he wants the truth to invade and transform every part of us. Quoting Isaiah, Jesus levels a blistering critique of religious leaders, claiming that while they know the Law, their "heart is far from me" (Mt 15:8). Cultural critic Antonio Gramsci warned of what he called the "intellectual's error," in which people think they can know something without feeling it. Art is uniquely used by God to engage us on *both* the intellectual and emotional levels. Thus, art moves us at a heart level.

Art scholars note that what makes the human artist unique is that not only do we treat sunsets, oceans, wildflowers, sunrises, or bustling cities as objects for art, but we treat ourselves as an object.

ROCKWELL PAINTING ROCKWELL

Norman Rockwell was a beloved American painter and illustrator who presented life in the United States by drawing simplistic but inviting characters. Some of his paintings made us laugh; others put us in a melancholic mood, longing for what America could be. He's most famous for the cover illustrations he did for the *Saturday Evening Post* that spanned five decades. When the *Post* was going to release excerpts of his autobiography, they presented him with an odd request: Would he paint himself? He agreed, and the result was a painting titled *Triple Self-Portrait*, where we see Rockwell sitting in front of a canvas containing a photo of himself taped to a corner. As he paints he both looks at the photo of himself and his own image in a mirror and replicates it on canvas. He's not the first to try it. In Rockwell's painting, in the upper corner of the canvas we see sketches of artists— Albrecht Dürer, Rembrandt van Rijn, Pablo Picasso, Vincent van Gogh—who also attempted to paint themselves. Rembrandt was so captivated by the idea that he produced more than ninety paintings of himself. Being self-reflective should not be taken for granted—it is a distinctly human trait. While a dog doesn't stop to reflect on how he's doing as a family pet, humans often reflect on how we are doing at being human.[3]

A key component of common grace is the ability humans have to not only assess our surroundings and other people but also to assess ourselves. What is my relationship with others? What do I expect out of life? Where do my expectations come from and are they realistic? What do I make of this lingering sense of discontent? How am I doing as a parent, spouse, or adult child of aging parents? Speaking of aging parents, what does it mean to age well? If Kustow is correct, then a key part of art is a revolt against the status quo in favor of a fresh perspective. The following areas will not only expose us to art that attempts to provide a new lens to see life but also provide conversation starters with our friends. With each illustration I'll connect it to a spiritual theme that allows us to take the conversation deeper.

Fresh Perspective on the Brevity of Life

One of the somber themes of Scripture is that our lives are fleeting. In vivid language biblical writers compare life to a short breath or our shadow we catch out of the corner of our eye (Ps 144:4). Faster than a runner, our lives sprint past us (Job 9:25). As our years come to an end, we let out a resigned sigh (Ps 90:9). The problem is, due to a life filled with to-do lists, degrees, kids, and career goals, we simply move unreflectively from point A to point B. Yes, life is short, but who has time to stop and think about the years zipping past us? The longer we live, the harder it is to ignore the years adding up. Midlife, notes philosopher Kieran Setiya, is a time where "the limited span of human life is no longer an abstraction."[4] When exactly does midlife come for most of us? According to the Centers for Disease Control and Prevention, we have roughly 78.6 years total. Obviously, life in a world of pandemics, disease, and accidents can greatly alter that number. But let's assume we represent the average. Therefore, for many of us midlife angst will occur in our late thirties or early forties. As my friends and family members gradually age, I like to periodically ask them what they think of the CDC's projection of longevity. Does it seem short? Does time seem to be moving fast?

One day at the martial arts school I attend, we students started talking about aging and the ever-present aches and pains that come with it. One person commented, "Well, aging is better than the alternative!" We all laughed. Whenever aging comes up or that life is zipping past us, I like to ask a question: What if life wasn't the seventy-eight years projected by the CDC but only eight days? The reaction is always one of shock. "That would be one bizarre world" is often the comment. I then describe one of the most thought-provoking short stories I've read.

LIFE IN A LITTLE MORE THAN A WEEK

"And he would live exactly eight days."[5] The chilling thought ushers us into a haunting world created by science-fiction writer Ray Bradbury. In *Frost and Fire* we encounter a civilization consisting of human survivors whose rocket ships crashed long ago on the brutal surface of a planet on the far side of our galaxy. These survivors live under the searing radiation of this obscure planet. An unexpected result is that those born on this planet have only eight days from birth to death. Under this acceleration, each day is the equivalent of ten years. "Birth was as quick as a knife. Childhood was over in a flash. Adolescence was a sheet of lighting. Manhood was a dream, maturity a myth, old age an inescapably quick reality, death a swift certainty."[6] The main character, Sim, is born into this world and struggles to embrace his dire circumstances. Until he hears of rumors that one rocket ship may not have been destroyed with the others. Perhaps, the rocket still works and escape is possible. *Imagine*, he thought, *living in a world where life didn't end in eight days but eighty years*. Eight days versus over twenty-nine thousand days—the decision seems simple. The problem is that it's a four-day journey to the rocket site—a journey that would take *half* of his life! Most think the journey is a fool's errand and that they should just enjoy life no matter how short. Sim is not convinced. Along with a companion he sets out to the hills to seek the rocket. They leave as adolescents and four days later arrive as aged adults. But they do arrive. And the rocket is functional. As they leave the atmosphere of the radiation-soaked planet, they soon feel the aging process slow. Sim has an overwhelming thought: *the nightmare is over.*

After I describe the story I like to ask what a person would do if in Sim's position? Would they spend half of their life seeking a rocket ship that may or may not exist? And if it does, what if it doesn't fly? They've spent half their life to get there, and it'll take the rest of it to get back to civilization. One question would determine their actions: Is risking eight days worth the possibility of gaining eighty years? Imagine a different scenario: Would you risk eighty years to gain life *without end*? With this story and these questions, I'm trying to find a way for my friends to ponder my favorite illustration about wrestling with the brevity of life: Pascal's wager. To me, Bradbury's story of Sim's quest allows me to transition to Pascal's view of life as a type of bet, or wager.

Spiritual Insight

This thought experiment is loved by some philosophers and hated by others. Over time, it has come to be known as *the wager*. Developed by Blaise Pascal in the 1600s, it's designed to help a person understand that—like Sim debating whether to pursue the rocket—you are using your life as a type of bet or wager. The wager focuses on how we should approach the ultimate question in life: Does God exist? The first option is to bet that God *does* exist and then live a life of devotion (seeking virtues like honesty, fidelity, and compassion, and casting off vices like dishonesty, infidelity, and meanness). If you are wrong and God doesn't exist, then you've not lost anything but have lived a virtuous life. The second option is to bet God *doesn't* exist. If you are wrong and he does, then you'll miss out on heaven and experience eternal separation from God and all you love. According to Pascal, it's the world's biggest no-brainer.

Clearly, you should bet on God existing because the potential gains (a good life on earth followed by eternal life with God) vastly outweigh potential losses (upon death discovering God exists, followed by eternal separation).

How does Pascal's thought experiment strike you? Do you agree with his conclusion that the only rational decision is to bet on God? Often my friends will comment that the wager—while interesting—is still a bet you can't be sure of. I agree. However, I present reasons why I'm betting on God and the evidence that pushes me to do so (signs of a Creator in nature, Jesus' amazing life, historical evidence of the resurrection, answers to prayer, a deep sense of Jesus' presence).[7]

Whenever discussing the wager, I make sure to bring up a point Pascal felt was essential: no one is sure how long they have to place a bet on God's existence. There are no guarantees you will reach the 78.6 years projected by the CDC. If life unexpectedly ends, the bet has been made for you. Pascal's goal is to motivate a person not to wait but rather to act today. In the pop song "If the World Was Ending," we meet a couple who has been separated for a year. They both experience a ground-shaking earthquake that causes them to ask, "If the world were ending, you'd come over, right?"[8] Knowing the clock was running out would hopefully motivate this couple to set aside differences and reconcile. Pascal would concur. Since no one knows how much time they have, a sense of urgency should move you to place a wager *today*!

GOING DEEPER

When sharing Pascal's wager, many forget to add a crucial element—how do you live out your bet once it's been cast in God's favor? If you are skeptical of God's existence but understand the rational thing to do is bet he is real, then you should also determine to live a life of devotion to him. For Pascal that means going to church, reading the Bible to get an accurate picture of God, praying, and exposing yourself to Christians who also have struggled to believe in God. C. S. Lewis spent years wrestling with the question of God. His nagging doubts were finally squelched by long dinner conversations with Christian friends such as J. R. R. Tolkien and Dorothy Sayers and praying to a God who might be there. When he finally cast his bet that God does exist, he described himself as the *most* reluctant convert in England.[9] Pascal's point is that, like Lewis, you can start a life of devotion to God even when you're not fully convinced he's real. As you do these Christian practices, Pascal was convinced you'll actually encounter the loving God and over time fully believe.[10]

Fresh Perspective on Our Longing for Love

In *The Four Loves*, C. S. Lewis explores the common words ancient Greeks used to differentiate forms of love: *philia* (love between friends), *agapē* (divine love), *storgē* (love between family), and *erōs* (romantic love).[11] Each is important, but they can greatly differ. For example, *erōs* is powerful romantic love that flares up quickly and expresses itself in dramatic ways; *philia* is often slow to develop but is durable.

One of the traps of today's culture is we easily become fixated on erotic love as seen in many of our favorite rom-coms. There's nothing wrong per se with erotic love; it just tends to dominate and overshadow the other forms. "When we watch a romantic movie or read a romance novel," notes psychologist Peter Stromberg, "the couple have a love for one another that is passionate and all-consuming."[12] It's the *all-consuming* part that concerns experts who study relationships. Why might fixating solely on eros be a problem? One of the concerns is that erotic love only tells *part* of the story. What happens when eros starts to fade and our fairy-tale romance faces reality?

INTO THE WOODS

In the quirky musical *Into the Woods* we reexamine our favorite fairy tales by asking, What comes next?[13] For instance, what happens after Jack kills the giant, steals the goose who lays golden eggs, and climbs down the beanstalk? It turns out that the giant was married and his equally gigantic wife climbs down the beanstalk and destroys Jack's village, exacting revenge. Concerning romantic love, what happens to Cinderella after her prince whisks her—golden slipper and all—to his opulent palace? The narrator begins Act 2 by stating, "Once upon a time . . . later." We soon learn the passionate love between Cinderella and the prince has waned. She's often left by herself as the prince scours the countryside performing his duties— including seducing other women. "After all, I am Prince Charming," he responds with a wry smile when confronted.

Stromberg notes, "If we are old enough to have had some long-term relationships, we very likely have also felt this overwhelming passion fade, to be replaced (in the best of cases) by feelings like love, affection, respect, friendship, and mutual attraction."[14] If a musical like *Into the Woods* can shed a fresh perspective on the dangers of eros, then art can also highlight the enduring power of eros undergirded by friendship (*philia*).

THIS IS US

In the hit TV series *This Is Us*, we are introduced to a couple—Rebecca and Jack—deeply immersed in eros.[15] After watching Rebecca sing in a bar, Jack's smitten. So is she, and almost as strangers they soon find themselves on a cross-country trip to pursue her dream to become a recording artist. Never mind that her parents completely object, and he's an unemployed Vietnam vet with undiagnosed PTSD. Eros seemingly conquers all. However, upon getting married she gives birth to triplets, with one being stillborn. While still at the hospital they learn a baby has been abandoned and dropped off at the front desk. Deeply moved, they decide to address their grief by adopting the baby. What follows is not merely a fixation on eros—which ebbs and flows and even comes crashing down during the series—but a deep-seated friendship that helps them face heartbreaking challenges. Their friendship keeps the family together and their love strong.

Spiritual Insight

Why are we so susceptible to the powerful pull of the all-encompassing nature of eros love? Simply put, we were created to be enveloped into the all-consuming love of the Father (*agapē*). Through common grace God puts a dissatisfaction into us that keeps us from making an idol of human love. "This longing," notes theologian Richard John Neuhaus, "is the source of the hunger and dissatisfaction that mark our lives." What do we hunger for: another one-night stand or something deeper? In addition to meeting Rebecca and Jack, we are also introduced through *This Is Us* to a stunningly handsome character named Kevin. As a model and movie star, he has his pick of women. Yet he's constantly dissatisfied with a life marked by sex, stardom, and drug use. Neuhaus would not be surprised. "The hunger is for nothing less than perfect communion with the One in whom all the fragments of our scattered existence come together."[16] Kevin, like our friends and neighbors, acutely feels this hunger but tries to satisfy it by fiercely pursuing eros. Common grace redirects this longing toward its original source—God.

GOING DEEPER

Evolution overkill is a term critics of evolution have coined to describe the odd yearning humans have to move past the mere impulse to survive. Evolution rests on a simple guiding principle that humans adapt to accomplish two things: survive and procreate—that's it. If that's so, then why "do humans compose symphonies, investigate quantum mechanics, and build cathedrals?"[17] Add to this the deep angst we often feel as we treat ourselves as an object of introspection: *Am I a good parent? What is the meaning of life? Have I picked the right career? Am I living a virtuous life? How can I make my surroundings not just safer but more beautiful?* Not only do these questions go far beyond the purview of natural selection, but they often produce emotional and intellectual discomfort. Yet we still ask them. Why?

Fresh Perspective on the Outcast

Even a cursory reading of the Scriptures shows God's concern for the poor or outcast. Not only do the poor find hope in God (Job 5:16), but helping them serves as a type of litmus test of our relationship with God. "He who oppresses the poor shows contempt for their Maker, but whoever is kind to the needy honors God" (Prov 14:31). Leaders of the ancient church took seriously God's disposition toward the marginalized. In a shocking passage James boldly asserts that pure or undefiled religion inherently entails caring for the down-and-out symbolized by orphans and widows (Jas 1:27). The problem is that in a world that shuns God's priorities, we easily get caught up in our own agendas. While those who lack financial stability are seen outside our favorite coffee shop or on a street corner during our daily commute, we get used to seeing them and easily ignore their pleas for help or their desperate stare. As Jewish author and mystic Martin Buber famously stated, we slowly adopt an *I-It relationship* to those in whom we no longer recognize humanity. This is unacceptable to God. Thus, he moves artists to take the perspective of the outcast.

One of our most important interpersonal skills is the ability to set aside our own perspective long enough to see the world through the eyes of another person. This ability—called perspective-taking—is more difficult for some than others. Scholars note that people brought up in cultures that value interconnectedness to fellow community members easily adopt the perspectives of others. "In contrast," notes researcher Boaz Keyser, "members of individualist cultures tend to strive for independence and have self-concepts defined in terms of their own aspirations and achievements."[18] In other words, it's easy for us to get immersed in our own little worlds. This was true of one artist who had slowly become numb to the screams of the homeless outside his apartment.

Traveling the world designing car interiors, Brian Peterson looked forward to coming home to Santa Ana, California, to rest and relax. But his peace was periodically interrupted by the disturbing screams of a homeless man outside his window. He was shocked at how easy it was for him and his wife to ignore it. "Oh, that's just the homeless guy, *again*." Until one day he went to talk to the man. During that conversation he saw the beauty of his homeless neighbor. He was so moved, he asked if he could paint a portrait of this man. This conversation and portrait lead to the "Faces of Santa Ana" project.

FACES OF SANTA ANA

The goal of the "Faces of Santa Ana" project is to change the perception we have of people living on the street. His first step was to remove the word *homeless* from our vocabulary. Those living on the street are not *homeless* but rather *people* experiencing homelessness. He paints these diverse individuals and then adds two key signatures. First, he signs it as the artist but then asks the subject of the painting to sign it as well. When asked to paint a mural in Santa Ana he chose not to include famous people from Hollywood or the vibrant LA crowd but those currently displaced. When Brian presents his portraits, he offers titles that challenge our perspective: *Daughter not a dealer* or *Neighbor instead of homeless*.[19]

Living in Southern California, where the homeless issue is a sobering reality, discussions are frequent among my neighbors. How should we respond? Whenever this topic arises, I show people the "Faces of Santa Ana" project on my cell phone and ask how we should treat people experiencing homelessness. I'm transparent in sharing how easy it is for me to adopt an I-It stance toward those working hard to make ends meet. Perhaps, part of fostering sympathy for others is to see life from their perspective.

Consider also an artist who didn't merely paint portraits on the side of walls but painted himself.

BLACK LIKE ME

How could a White journalist understand the deep segregation experienced by many African Americans in the late 1950s? In an extreme form of perspective-taking, John Howard Griffin—under the care of a dermatologist— took doses of a drug that slowly darkened his skin. In addition, for one week he spent fifteen hours a day under an ultraviolet lamp to complete the process. Once his White friends were fooled by his transformation, thinking he was a Black man, John spent six weeks traveling through the Deep South. He immediately noticed what he called the "hate stare" from Whites. An unexpected challenge was constantly looking for a restroom that did not have a "Whites Only!" sign over the doorway. Griffin lived in constant fear of soiling himself or being arrested for relieving himself in public since colored restrooms were few and far between. Not all the negativity came from Whites. During a bus trip he gave up his seat for a White woman and noticed disapproving looks from Black passengers. Then after the six weeks ended and his White pigmentation returned, John experienced death threats from those who thought his project was obscene. Being forced to flee his family to Mexico for protection, he concluded his book with a plea: "If we could only put ourselves in the shoes of others to see how we would react, then we might become aware of the injustice of discrimination and the tragic inhumanity of every kind of prejudice."[20]

Spiritual Insight

The subtitle of the first edition of Howard's book *Black Like Me* surely was meant to be provocative: "A White Man Learns to Live the Life of a Negro by Becoming One." While attention-grabbing, it's simply not true. Regardless of what you think of Howard's project, he never stopped being a White person; changing his skin tone did not alter his ethnicity. In contrast, when Jesus came to our planet, he didn't merely slap on human flesh to hide his divinity. While the Scriptures are clear that all of divinity rests in Jesus (Col 2:9), he was fully human. He began as a fetus and was born a helpless infant of frail human parents. Subsequently, he knew firsthand what it's like to grow tired from work, feel grief at the death of a friend, be unjustly judged, fear his own death, and feel abandoned by friends and even God. "We do not have a high priest who is unable to em-pathize with our weaknesses," asserts Hebrews 4:15. The Greek word for empathy (*sympatheō*) connotes knowledge by way of common experience, leading Greek expert Kenneth Wuest to conclude that "our Lord's appreciation of our infirmities is an experiential one."[21] Jesus knows the human condition—one filled with pain and sorrow—because it happened to *him*!

Conclusion

Released in 1971, "What's Going On?" was selected by *Rolling Stone* magazine as the fourth-greatest song ever recorded. The song starts with Marvin Gaye acknowledging the tears of mothers and brothers nationwide. The song was spurred on by the turmoil of the Vietnam War abroad and violent antiwar protests at home. The haunting refrain asks, "What's going on?" The song struck a chord with listeners and is still relevant today. Reflecting on the song, Gaye commented that he wanted to touch the souls of his listeners: "I wanted them to take a look at what was happening in the world."[22] God wants the same. Common grace, propelled by artists of every stripe, forces us to see the world in fresh and often uncomfortable ways that cause us to equally ask, What's going on?

Further Reading

Brian Godawa, *Hollywood Worldviews: Watching Films with Wisdom and Discernment* (Downers Grove, IL: InterVarsity Press, 2009).

Philip Graham Ryken, *Art for God's Sake: A Call to Recover the Arts* (P&R Publishing: Phillipsburg, NJ, 2006).

CHAPTER FOUR

Communication

LIFE-GIVING WORDS IN TODAY'S ARGUMENT CULTURE

America is in crisis.

The crisis is felt across gender, racial, and ethnic lines. Young and old, wealthy and poor, religious and nonreligious are equally at risk. It predates #MeToo, Covid-19, and Black Lives Matter. In fact, this crisis makes talking about issues nearly impossible.

The crisis we are facing?

Incivility.

For the past twenty years Americans have identified a lack of civility as an issue that threatens the health of our workplaces, neighborhoods, and families. At a time when it seems we can't agree on anything, 98 percent of Americans state that incivility is a serious problem; while 68 percent agree it's reached crisis levels. From cyberbullying to hate speech to workplace harassment to verbal abuse and intolerance, the vast majority of us (87 percent) no longer feel safe in public places.[1]

What are we to make of such disconcerting statistics? Our level of incivility has even a new term: *Thunderdome communication.*

WELCOME TO THE THUNDERDOME

In the third installment of the cult classic *Mad Max* trilogy, a young Mel Gibson plays an unlikely hero in an apocalyptic world where communities compete and kill for ever-decreasing energy sources. He's captured by the cruel dictator Aunty Entity (played by Tina Turner) of a small colony fueled by methane gas. To appease her subjects, Aunty Entity has created her own version of the Roman gladiatorial games called, the Thunderdome. There are no rules, only a fight to the death. Before each contest, the dictator announces: "Two men enter, one man leaves." Crowds cheer as two people tear each other apart![2]

Today, communication theorists have borrowed this movie reference and applied it to how we approach our disagreements. This particularly applies to our political disagreements or what some call "Thunderdome politics." This political vitriol was evident during President Trump's February 2020 State of the Union Address when he famously failed to shake the outstretched hand of his political rival Nancy Pelosi—leaving her hand dangling midair. Her response? As the president finished his speech, Pelosi publicly ripped up a transcript of the speech page by page. The next day, supporters from each party defended their leader while demonizing the actions of the other.[3] Welcome to the Thunderdome!

While we are all concerned about incivility, what can we do about it? Recently, I've been asking friends if there is any way out of our Thunderdome approach to disagreements. If things are to change, what needs to happen? Since I teach communication, I'm often asked for my opinion of where to start. I suggest we need to come to terms with both the essential role communication plays in our well-being and how to reclaim the power of words. As the conversation develops, hopefully those we engage will see how God's common grace has been at work to help us adopt a view of communication that can bring fractured communities together.

The Necessity of Communication

One way to recover an appreciation of communication is to imagine if we could no longer connect or communicate with people. Reuel Howe, in his classic book *The Miracle of Dialogue*, writes, "Dialogue is to love, what blood is to the body. When the flow of blood stops, the body dies."[4] Equally, asserts Howe, when dialogue or human connection stops, we put ourselves—bodies, minds, and souls—at great risk. Consider these sobering realities:

- People who lack strong relationships have two or three times the risk of early death, regardless of whether they smoke, drink alcoholic beverages, or exercise regularly.

- Terminal cancer strikes socially isolated people more often than those who have close personal relationships.

- Divorced, separated, and widowed people are five to ten times more likely to need mental hospitalization than their married counterparts.

- Social isolation is a major risk factor contributing to coronary disease, comparable to physiological factors such as diet, cigarette smoking, obesity, and lack of physical exercise.[5]

GOING DEEPER

In his provocative book *Sapiens: A Brief History*, historian Yuval Noah Harari asserts that in our 13.7 billion years of history human cultures only began to take form seventy thousand years ago. In those thousands of years three pivotal revolutions have occurred. The Cognitive Revolution (complex thinking, problem solving, reflection), the Agricultural Revolution (adapting to seasons, creation of tools, harnessing the power of animals), and the Scientific Revolution (creating hypotheses, developing elaborate means of verification, discovering complex natural laws). While Harari's timeline is a matter of debate, the three revolutions he identified most certainly occurred. While each could be considered salient examples of common grace, all three revolutions are dependent on human communication. For example, the Agricultural Revolution would never have happened unless humans could formulate thoughts (self-talk) and share discoveries with fellow farmers (interpersonal communication). Without the ability to communicate each would be left to their limited discoveries. While we often take communication for granted, it's part of God's common grace that we can connect through elaborate forms of verbal and nonverbal means.

The desperate need for communication and connection is seen in the blockbuster movie *Cast Away*.

A CASTAWAY'S GREATEST THREAT

Chuck Noland (played by Tom Hanks) is a workaholic who solves shipping problems for FedEx. On Christmas Eve he's called away to Malaysia to addresses a crisis that could cost the company significant money. However, the FedEx cargo plane he's flying on crashes in the Pacific Ocean leaving Noland the sole survivor. He washes up on a deserted island and faces the challenge of building a fire, hunting, creating a shelter, and even performing basic medical procedures such as removing an abscessed tooth. Over time, he comes to realize that his greatest challenge is a lack of human connection. His isolation soon fuels thoughts of suicide. One day, he discovers a box has washed up on shore from the cargo plane. It contains a Wilson Sporting Goods volleyball, which will soon become the key to his survival. After placing a bloody palm print on it to serve as a crude face, he names the ball Wilson and constantly talks to it during the rest of the film. Every action Noland takes is carefully narrated to this odd inanimate partner. This communication—even though one-sided—saves his life.[6]

The need for intimate human connection is not limited to castaways but rather seems to be universally hardwired in us from the beginning. In the Genesis narrative we learn that after surveying creation, God affirmed that all was good (Gen 1:31). However, after creating Adam, God determined not everything was good or complete. Why? Adam had resources (the garden), a purpose (caretaking of his environment), and most importantly access to God. Yet something was off. God responds that it "is not good for the man to be *alone*" (Gen 2:18, emphasis

added). Only when Adam connects with his counterpart—
Eve—is he deemed complete or good. A significant part of that
connection is how the man and woman converse with each other,
as evidenced by Adam's verbal proclamation to Eve that she is
"flesh of my flesh" (Gen 2:23).

The Bible isn't the only authority to assert the idea that communication is central to our humanity. A similar conclusion was
reached by Oxford scholar and researcher Theodore Zeldin
after he interviewed eighteen women from diverse geographical
locations. Each woman—though separated by economic, ethnic,
educational, and geographical differences—equally found communication to be the *most* life-giving factor.[7] Where did this
desire to use communication to connect with others come from?
Via common grace God implanted a desire to use communication for connection rather than division.

Again, I am merely offering one possible explanation for this
desire to intimately converse and connect with others. As the
conversation turns to other aspects of the power of communication, we'll uncover more signs of God's common grace.

GOING DEEPER

What if our desire for human connection resulted in
rebellion against God? Could language be used to
solidify our opposition to God? After the flood, God's
heart is again broken as he witnesses Noah's descen-
dants coming together to build a tower so magnificent
that it will reach into heaven, resulting in humans believing they are on par with God. God's response is unique,
and the Tower of Babel narrative continues to have
ramifications today. God decides to scatter people and

"confuse their language" so they cannot easily conspire (Gen 11:6). This judgment shows God's mercy in that while this confusion of language separates large populations—such as nations—from easily plotting against God, it still allows intimate connection within individual nations, communities, and families. God is not done reforming human language. In the consummated kingdom, every tribe, tongue, and nation will be reunited in harmony—sharing the same mode of communication (Rev 7:9)![8]

Power of Communication

Long before Mad Max and Thunderdome communication, God moved ancient Jewish writers to explore the peril and promise of communication. "The tongue" notes these Jewish thinkers, "has the power of life and death" (Prov 18:21). These writers do not shy away from both possibilities. Before sharing with others what these ancient writers thought about communication, I like to ask them to give examples of the way speech can tear down or build up people. One fellow mountain-bike rider, a successful lawyer, shocked me by confessing, "I was once told by a family relative that I was dumb. I was only seven at the time, but I've *never* forgotten it." Can you relate? Each of us can remember words that built us up or tore at our self-esteem. When the time is right, I share with them different sayings from a body of Jewish Wisdom literature we know as the book of Proverbs.

Imparting death. Using vivid metaphors, these ancient writers describe the potentially devastating power of words. Reckless words are presented as a piercing sword (Prov 12:18). A word spoken in the wrong way can "break a bone" (Prov 25:15). A person's spirit is easily crushed by a deceitful tongue (Prov 15:4). In plotting evil, a scoundrel's speech is like a "scorching fire" (Prov 16:27). Not only can negative words separate close friends (Prov 16:28), but a whole city can be disrupted by mockery (Prov 29:8). Old Testament scholar David Hubbard argues that what these ancient writers want most for us to understand about language is that the tongue is "literally a lethal weapon—to others and ourselves."[9]

One particular proverb is worth noting. Just as the "north wind" can bring driving rain, so a "sly tongue" *evokes* an angry response (Prov 25:23). The caustic words we use often evoke or solicit caustic words in return. Communication scholars identify such a response as a *negative communication spiral*, in which our negative actions prompt others to respond in kind. It's a lesson a TV mom learned the hard way.

CHRISTMAS TURNED UGLY

Malcolm in the Middle humorously follows the adventures of a lovable dysfunctional family. It enjoyed a six-year run and launched the careers of Frankie Muniz, Jane Kaczmarek, and Bryan Cranston. In one episode the mother, Lois, is trying to finish last-minute Christmas shopping and sits in her car outside a mall checking her list. A woman next to her—arms filled with gifts—accidentally hits Lois's car door with her door. "Excuse me," replies a perturbed Lois, "I know you didn't think anyone would catch you, but you just slammed your door into my car! The least you could do is say you're sorry!" Her accusatory tone evokes a sharp reply. "You don't have to take that tone," tersely replies the stranger. "It's not like I'm hurting your resale value!" Angered even more, Lois purposefully opens her door, hitting the stranger's car. "Oops,

sorry!" she says with a smirk. In response the woman sur-
veys the damage to her car and slams her door—twice—
into Lois's car. What ensues is both women driving like
demolition-derby drivers in the parking lot ramming each
other. At one point the camera focuses on Lois's bumper
sticker: "War Is Not the Answer!" To the horror of fellow
Christmas shoppers, these two women are caught in a
negative spiral that destroys both cars.[10]

The central feature of a negative communication spiral is that
a person doesn't merely respond in kind but increases the
intensity—You hit my door. I'll hit yours twice! Thus, a raised
voice is met with a shout, and an angry tone is met with pro-
fanity. These devastating spirals can cause significant harm to
our self-esteem or identity. Why do words so deeply affect us?
Cultural studies scholar Judith Butler asks a provocative
question: "Could language injure us if we were not, in some
sense, linguistic beings who require language in order to be?"[11]
Butler is suggesting that the view we have of ourselves—our
self-image—has been formed by the words spoken to us both
positive and negative. Some researchers have even adopted a
term, *the Michelangelo phenomenon*, to express how our interaction with others emotionally sculpts our impression of who
we are and how we view ourselves.

THE MICHELANGELO PHENOMENON

While still in his early twenties, Michelangelo spent two
years sculpting his masterpiece *David* from a massive
block of white marble. The seventeen-foot-tall statue of
King David has been described by art experts worldwide
as *the* perfect sculpture. However, the marble slab he

used was hardly perfect. Having been abandoned for over forty years, it had significantly deteriorated and included a crude chisel mark. However, through Michelangelo's masterful skill, the marble was transformed into something beautiful. Psychologists assert the same happens to us via words. Just as the original slab of marble used by Michelangelo had a chisel mark in it that disfigured it, so a negative word can warp our self-perception. But just as the slab of marble was transformed into a work of art, so positive words and affirmations can positively transform our self-perception.[12]

Since we are all linguistic beings chiseled by the words of others, we must appreciate the power our words have on those we meet. Even people we may think are impervious to criticism and the power of words are susceptible to the Michelangelo phenomenon. Consider a woman who seemingly has everything.

SEXIEST WOMAN ALIVE WARNING ON NEGATIVE WORDS

Not only has Megan Fox been in blockbuster movies like *The Transformers*, but she was named—at the age of twenty-one—the world's sexiest woman. The organizer of the worldwide poll that crowned her said of Fox, "She's young, she's hot, she's a rising star and her sex appeal has transformed this year's list. She's got a great future ahead of her." Certainly, Fox is impervious to criticism or a negative review. Not so. During an interview, Fox candidly admitted how much words hurt and the toll they've taken on her. "We have to be careful with our words—they're powerful. That's something I wish most people would understand. We live in a culture where it's a game to be the most hateful to get the most attention. You're speaking words over real people, who are permeable, who have hearts. Your negativity can influence them. Those things affect me really deeply."[13]

As negative communication spirals pick up in intensity, not only does harshness increase but we begin to eliminate other words from our vocabulary such as *gentleness*. Communication scholar Perry Glanzer searched academic journals in the past three decades to see how much they explored the virtue of gentleness. "I did not find one," he notes. How might our academic neglect of this virtue trickle down to our everyday usage of the word? "Indeed, if one is to trust the Google n-gram, the use of the word 'gentle' is at its lowest point in the last 300 years. Microsoft Word even suggests that I change gentlemen to 'men' or 'people.' Based on these trends, it appears our society thinks we no longer have use for gentleness."[14]

A key part of common grace as related to language is our ability to do what communication scholars label as *feedforward*. Central to feedforward is our ability to anticipate how our communication will affect others. Will the words I put in this text antagonize the person reading it? Will my comments in the chat section further the conversation or derail it? To fail to anticipate our actions can have disastrous outcomes. To drive home my point, I like to share two illustrations.

GENDER REVEAL GONE WRONG

It was supposed to be a special day. A couple gathered their closest friends and family to reveal the gender of their upcoming birth. Their plan seemed simple: a smoke-emitting pyrotechnic device sends out pink or blue smoke and everyone cheers! What they didn't anticipate

was that in addition to the smoke, the machine also emit-
ted small sparks that landed on brush and grass dried
out by years of drought. It took only seconds for a wildfire to start that would consume over twenty-two thousand acres and force massive evacuations. A curt message issued by fire officials flatly stated, "Those
responsible for starting fires due to negligence or illegal
activity can be held financially and criminally
responsible."[15] The failure to anticipate would cause
massive hardship for surrounding communities.

I combine that illustration with one used by a New Testament
writer who asserts we are equally responsible for the verbal
wildfires our words can cause. James describes our tongues as a
type of deadly fire (Jas 3:6). Reminiscent of the wildfire that
destroyed thousands of acres, he asks us to consider "how great
a forest is set on fire" by a spark from the tongue (Jas 3:5). The
fire he's referring to isn't dried-out brush or grass but a rela-
tional fire that divides friends and communities. When James
says we ought to *consider* the damage done by our tongues, he's
asking us to engage in feedforward and to monitor our harmful
communication.

God didn't only use common grace to give us a vision of the
destructive power of words, but he also gives us an idea of how
words can heal. The Michelangelo phenomenon goes both
ways—while our words can undoubtedly cause damage, they
can also positively shape us.

GOING DEEPER

In Proverbs 6 we encounter a remarkable list of what God hates. The word *hate* is a Hebrew word often associated with disgust and represents God's emotional reaction to certain human actions. Seven actions evoke disgust from God: "haughty eyes, a lying tongue, hands that shed innocent blood, a heart that devises wicked schemes, feet that are quick to shed evil, a false witness who pours out lies, and a person who stirs up conflict in the community" (Prov 6:17-19). It's interesting that of the seven mentioned four have to do with our communication. "Haughty eyes" refers to an arrogant stance toward others, as evidenced by a nonverbal posture meant to intimidate and demean others. A lying tongue and false witness both pour out lies. Last, God reacts to anyone who uses communication to foster conflict among individuals. The first step toward respecting communication is to realize the emotional response speech acts elicit from God. Far from being a stoic deity, God is deeply moved by our verbal and nonverbal choices.

Imparting life. The same Jewish writers who warned us of the negative power of words also vividly state their positive influence. Gentle words are a tree of life (Prov 15:4) and "kind words" are compared to honey that is "sweet to the soul and healthy to the bones" (Prov 16:24).

Words can dramatically change how we see ourselves. A powerful transformation is seen in the bestselling book *The Help*.

NEVER FORGET, YOU IS . . .

Set in the early 1960s in Jackson, Mississippi, Kathryn
Stockett's novel *The Help* tells the story of Eugenia
"Skeeter" Phelan, who returns home to write about her
Southern town. What she discovers is a town enveloped
in racial power dynamics where African American women
help clean houses and raise the owner's White children.
We also discover that White women must fit into an ideal-
ized view of femininity that is, above all, refined and thin.
Aibileen Clark is a Black servant assigned to a family with
an overweight, clumsy young daughter. Every day this
girl's mother tells her to stand up straight and stop eating
so much. It breaks Aibileen's heart to hear such crushing
words falling on young ears. To counteract them she
waits until the mother is absent. Sitting in a rocker with
the girl resting in her lap, Aibileen recites these words,
"You is kind. You is smart. You is important." Over and
over, they say these words together. With each word the
girl's face lights up. Each day, that is their secret routine—
one designed to be honey to a little girl's soul.[16]

"Sure," your friend says, "kids are moldable. I just wish that
worked as easily on adults." Your friend raises a good question:
Do positive words equally affect adults? The results of a unique
student art project that went viral suggest adults are equally
susceptible to the power of affirming words.

PHOTO OF SOMETHING BEAUTIFUL

In 2017, a psychology student in Belgium came up with a
unique senior project. He wanted to see how strangers
reacted to being called "beautiful." How would you react? In the middle of a majestic public square in

Brussels—filled with jaw-dropping architecture, fountains, and art—he walked up to strangers and asked if he could take their picture for a university project. Participants didn't realize he was already filming them through his camera. When asked what the project was about, he told them he was instructed to take a picture of something beautiful, and he chose this person. Some participants laughed, others smiled, and almost all blushed. Some even tried to talk him into taking a picture of something else. But *everyone* came alive. In the video we see life being spoken into these participants. Years later, another student wondered if he could get a similar reaction from people, but not limit it to one geographic location. He took months taking photos of diverse people who were told they were beautiful. From Japan to France to Turkey to Spain to Africa to the United States, he received an almost universal response—joy.[17]

Is it possible God has hardwired us so that positive words create a strong reaction in our brains? Some researchers say our brains receive compliments in the same way we react to being given money. In one study, forty-eight adults were recruited for an experiment in which they had to complete a particular task. Once finished, they were broken into three groups. The first group received specific compliments from those running the study. The second group merely watched the first group receive the compliments but didn't receive any themselves. The last group had no idea compliments were being given but were merely asked to evaluate their own performance. The next day the three groups again performed similar tasks. The group that had previously received praise from researchers *vastly* outperformed the other two groups. The lead researcher, Norihiro Sadata, noted,

"To the brain, receiving a compliment is as much a social reward as being rewarded money. . . . There seems to be scientific validity behind the message 'praise to encourage improvement.'"[18]

A Universal Appreciation of Words

Reclaiming the inherent power of words is crucial to addressing the crisis of incivility felt by most of us. The book of Proverbs is full of cautions concerning our use of words. Did God give this insight to Jewish writers alone, or via common grace did he pass on that insight to thinkers and writers across the world throughout history? This last illustration shows that God seems to have planted an appreciation of the power of words in people from vastly different worldviews.

- *Hinduism.* Nearly 15 percent (1.1 billion) of the world's population follow the teachings of Hindu scriptures and teachers. One Hindu writer notes that Hinduism not only appreciates the power of words but offers a clue to what causes us to harm others verbally: "Words can comfort or hurt. It is our pride that makes us use words that hurt."[19]

- *Buddha.* Christian apologist Peter Kreeft asserts that if you were to take a poll asking people to identify the most popular and deepest thinker of all time, next to Jesus people would say the Buddha. Nearly 470 million people worldwide follow his teachings—including his belief that words have the potential to change the world: "Words have the power to both destroy and heal. When words are both true and kind, they can change our world."[20]

- *Muhammad.* Muhammad was selected by historian Michael Hart as *the* most influential person in human history. Not only is he the founder of Islam but also the sole author of the Qur'an, a book that gives guidance to millions. In the thirty-third sura or chapter, he writes that followers of Allah should only seek to "speak righteous words."[21]

- *Confucius.* Confucius, China's most famous teacher, philosopher, and political theorist, whose ideas have influenced the civilization of East Asia and beyond, asserts that without a knowledge of the power of words, future wisdom will be fleeting: "Without knowing the force of words, it is impossible to know more."[22]

- *Luther Standing Bear.* Though not sharing the renown of Buddha or Muhammad, Lakota chief Luther Standing Bear is notable in American history as one of the first Native American educators and philosophers of the twentieth century. His insight is relevant for a modern world immersed in constant electronic communication: "Silence is the mother of truth, for the silent man is ever to be trusted, while the man ever ready with speech was never taken seriously."[23]

- *Sam Harris.* The role words play in addressing the human predicament is not regulated to the spiritually-minded. As a committed atheist, popular writer Sam Harris is no friend of religion, but he too is convinced of the role our words will play in solving current problems. "All we have to solve our problems is conversations. It's either conversation or violence."[24]

What's to be made of this universal appreciation of the awesome power of words? I like to point out that not only do these diverse thinkers share the same view of the efficacy of words that the writers of Proverbs did, but some share an eerie similarity in their phraseology. For example, the Buddha's claim that "Words have the power to both destroy and heal" is almost a paraphrase of Jewish writers asserting that "The tongue has the power of life and death" (Prov 18:21). Yet it's highly unlikely that the Buddha—living in what is now modern-day Nepal sometime during the fifth to fourth centuries BC—had access to any written portion of the Old Testament. Nevertheless, the truth expressed therein deeply resonated with him. Is it possible that God, knowing a world in rebellion would use words as weapons, planted a vision of how words could heal?

When discussing the power of our language choices, I find it useful to bring up a key quote from Jesus. After all, he was ranked as the third most influential person in human history by historian Michael Hart. In the Gospels, Jesus makes a somber statement that each of us will have to give an account for the words we used while living on earth (Mt 12:36). Can you imagine having to account for the millions of words we have spoken? Why are our words so important? Christ explains, "The mouth speaks what the heart is full of" (Mt 12:34). For biblical writers the heart represents the center of a person's personality, including emotions, intellect, and volition. Jesus is suggesting that through our communication with others we glean a robust picture of a person's true self. What does our current crisis of incivility—and the words we use to demonize each other—tell us about our heart condition? Perhaps we are spiritually sick. If so, what remedies are available to us?

GOING DEEPER

The fact that all people—Christian and non-Christians alike—receive common grace poses an interesting question: Can Christ-followers learn from the insights of a Buddha or Confucius? Christian philosophers J. P. Moreland and Francis Beckwith answer in the affirmative. "Repeatedly, Scripture acknowledges the wisdom of cultures outside of Israel; for example, the Phoenicians (Zech. 9:2) and many others. The remarkable achievements produced by human wisdom are acknowledged in Job 28:1-11." They assert we "must never forget that God is the God of creation and general revelation just as he is the God of Scripture and special revelation."[25] Their conclusion is supported by the famous traveling preacher and theologian John Wesley, who cautioned fellow Christians that to "imagine none can teach you but those who are themselves saved from sin is a very great and dangerous mistake. Give not place to it for a moment."[26] While no doubt Christians must always check the insights of others with the teaching of Scripture, we can be open to learning from insights of thinkers who have been guided by God's common grace.[27]

Conclusion

During the time of Christ, Roman philosophers taught *talis oratio, quails vita* ("As the speech, so the life"). They cautioned that the quality of our speech is an indicator of the quality of our private and public lives. What was true then equally applies to us today. In a nation marred by incivility that has reached crisis proportions and threatens our very way of life, we'd do well to listen to these ancient thinkers. Our language choices today are driving us apart and keeping us from talking about issues of race, immigration, and politics. To change our speech we'll first have to embrace an idea of what virtuous speech sounds like and how speaking death is counter to that image. We are indebted to God, who has given us—through spokespeople such as Buddha, Muhammad, Confucius, Sitting Bear, Sam Harris, Jesus, and Jewish proverb writers—a vision of life-giving speech that can draw us together. If not, our collective lives will more and more mirror our vitriol.

Further Reading

Tim Muehlhoff and Todd Lewis, *Authentic Communication: Christian Speech Engaging Culture*, Christian Worldview Integration, ed. J. P. Moreland and Francis Beckwith (Downers Grove, IL: InterVarsity Press, 2010).

Quentin Schultze, *Communicating with Grace and Virtue* (Grand Rapids, MI: Baker, 2020).

CHAPTER FIVE

War

LESSENING OUR ABILITY TO KILL

Homo homini lupus.

For those needing to brush up on your Latin, this phrase translates "Man is a wolf to man." Though its exact origin is unclear, it existed long before the time of Christ and was quoted by Roman playwrights and philosophers such as Seneca. Like wolves in the wild, we quickly turn on each other. This turning is often expressed in an activity as old as humans—war.

"The dawn of history," notes historians Ernst and Trevor Dupuy, "and the beginning of organized warfare went hand in hand."[1] As soon as stones were used for digging, they were quickly converted into crude weapons. In his haunting documentary *War*, Gwynne Dyer notes that a primary function of early societies was a constant preparation to either protect themselves or attack others. He concludes: "We must consider an unwelcome possibility: that war is the inevitable accompaniment of any human civilization."[2]

Imagine how heartbreaking it must have been for God to see humans use our creativity to produce more and more effective killing tools and strategies. The creation mandate to be fruitful and multiply inextricably has been linked to war-making. The big picture of God's reaction to war and violence can fit into what theologians call a *creation-fall-redemption* framework.[3] At the creation of the first humans common grace allowed us to foster harmony, communicate with kindness, create tools to help with harvests, and intimately worship God. At the fall our unity with fellow image-bearers became marred by coveting what others have, territorialism, creating weapons of war, and enmity with God. The world is thrown into a destructive spiral where evil begets evil and the good gifts God has provided are often warped and used to dominate others. God's response is the focus of this book—he continues to give good gifts to help us cope with a world gone wrong. The good news is that ultimately God is redeeming us; then universal shalom will be restored. In his euphoric vision John envisions a world where crying, mourning, and pain are gone and people live in harmony as coinhabitants of a glorious city (Rev 21:1-4). God himself will dwell with us and we will rest under his shalom (v. 3). Until then we search for signs of God's grace that help us pursue peace in a world bent on war. Not only do we discover God's grace, but we also find ways to communicate it to our neighbors, friends, and coworkers.

Every time we open our computers and check our favorite news source, we are met with disturbing stories of life in war-torn countries and acts of violence between citizens. No doubt this will surface questions from those around us who know we are religious. "Why doesn't God just end war? Doesn't he care?"

is a constant refrain. These are good questions that deserve answers. Such questions force me to ask my own questions: How does God view war and violence, and what is he doing about it? If God hates war so much, then why did he seemingly engage in it himself via the armies of Israel?

How God Views Violence and War

In unflinching language God states that he hates "hands that shed innocent blood" (Prov 6:16-17). Those who "put an innocent or honest person to death" surely will not be acquitted from divine judgment (Ex 23:7). Therefore, the children of Israel were prohibited from doing "violence to the resident alien" (Jer 22:3 ESV). When they ignore this command, God delivers a scathing rebuke to the people of Israel through the prophet Isaiah:

> Their deeds are evil deeds,
>> and acts of violence are in their hands.
> Their feet rush into sin;
>> they are swift to shed innocent blood.
> They pursue evil schemes;
>> acts of violence mark their ways.
> The way of peace they do not know. (Is 59:6-8)

Amid such violence the prophet reminds us that the "arm of the LORD is not too short to save, nor his ear too dull to hear" (Is 59:1).

If God hates war and violence so much, why not get rid of it? This question was posed to me after watching a powerful antiwar movie. I have a group of friends who recommend movies that we all watch and then meet to discuss. One movie we watched has stayed with me. When released in the United States it was the *most*-watched movie on basic cable in 1984. *Threads* is a disturbing and unflinching depiction of the aftereffects of a nuclear attack on a sleepy working-class town in Sheffield, England. Be warned, it is not for the faint of heart.

When we met to discuss it, one person acknowledged I was religious and asked, "Isn't God big enough to stop war?" I affirmed that it was a good question. I then asked him how God might specifically end war. "Well, a good place to start is to get rid of all weapons like nukes. No weapons, no war," he replied. The other people in the group nodded in agreement. I gently pushed back and explained that I wasn't so sure getting rid of weapons would deal with our propensity toward war and violence. I then shared a fascinating short story by the science-fiction master Ray Bradbury. In "A Piece of Wood," we are privy to an eerie conversation between a soldier and a high-ranking military official—one that could change the history of the world.

A WORLD WITHOUT WEAPONS

A soldier sits at a general's desk and shockingly reveals that he's created a machine that can instantly rust and render useless the metal common to all weapons. Thus, if used on the guns, tanks, fighter planes, aircraft carriers, and bullets and bombs, they will be reduced to a pool of metallic powder. The general thinks he's just messing with him. But what if it did exist? counters the soldier. The general shifts in his seat and mulls over the possibility. He then issues a frightening response. Such a machine wouldn't make any difference. None. If humans were deprived of weapons, it wouldn't stop war because we'd simply beat each other to death with fists if necessary. "And, if you cut off their hands they'd use their feet to stomp each other. And if you cut their legs off they'd spit on each other. And if you cut off their tongues and stopped their mouths with corks they'd fill the atmosphere so full of hate that mosquitoes would drop to the ground and birds would fall dead from telephone wires."[4] Resolved, the soldier gets up to leave. As the door closes, the general notices metallic dust at his feet—his sidearm has rusted and evaporated. In a rage he smashes his wooden desk chair against the wall. Seizing one of the broken legs the general runs out after the soldier. *A piece of wood is all I need to kill him,* he mutters to himself.

I asked the group what they thought of the general's stark assessment of life without weapons. Would a weaponless world stop us from treating each other as wolves or merely force us to adapt? Though God hates war, he understands that violence resides deep in the human heart. Philosopher Thomas Hobbes—from a secular perspective—shockingly asserts that the state of nature is characterized by the "war of every man against every man."[5] Therefore, God prompts us to decide to end war and turn to him. "It is worth noting that the whole point of Christianity," explains J. B. Phillips, "lies not in interference with the human power to choose, but in producing a willing consent to choose good rather than evil."[6]

Rather than revoking our power to choose and *forcing* us to end violence, God prods us, via common grace, to treat each other in humane ways. But how? In a world of violence where often it's every person against the other, how can we curb our taste for war?

GOING DEEPER

While God understands that merely getting rid of weapons will not remove the violence in our hearts, it is fascinating to read what will be the fate of instruments designed to hurt and kill. The psalmist writes that one day God will be fully exalted, as evidenced by a cessation of war, and the nations will watch as "he breaks the bow and shatters the spear; he burns the shields with fire" (Ps 46:9). The prophet Isaiah offers a powerful vision where people under God's rule will "beat their swords into plowshares and their spears into pruning hooks" (Is 2:4). In another passage the prophet asserts,

> Every warrior's boot used in battle
>   and every garment rolled in blood
> will be destined for burning,
>   will be fuel for the fire. (Is 9:5)

If this is God's reaction to ancient weapons made of stone and steel, what must his reaction be to weapons of mass destruction that can destroy our entire world many times over?

Putting Limits on War

While the Scriptures state that one day swords will be turned into plowshares, that day has not yet come. In the meantime God helps us envision not only the carnage of unrestrained war but also ideas of how to make war less destructive.

Unleash the dogs of war. This phrase, uttered by Mark Anthony in Shakespeare's play *Julius Caesar*, has come to serve as a timeless warning: once war is unleashed, you may not be able to reel it back. "War is not like a sport that can be quickly stopped at the blow of a whistle and its repercussions last for generations."[7] A key gift God has given us is hypothetical thinking in which we not only focus on what *is* but also what *could be* under certain situations. When it comes to making war, this gift of common grace is crucial to helping us envision how easily things can slip away from us in a world rigged for war. In such a tenuous world, war could be triggered by something seemingly innocuous as colorful balloons.

99 RED BALLOONS

Seven years before the Berlin Wall crumbled in 1989, musician Carlo Karges attended a Rolling Stones concert in West Berlin. He noticed red balloons being released by concertgoers and watched them float over the wall into communist-controlled East Berlin. How would these innocent balloons be perceived on radar, and could they be seen as a threat? If so, how would the East German military respond? Karges took this hypothetical situation and wrote a powerful antiwar song titled "99 Red Balloons."[8] In the song, lazily floating balloons are interpreted by generals as a threat that not only promotes panic but also causes the "war machine" to "spring to life." Quickly, ninety-nine war ministers gather and order ninety-nine fighter jets to attack a neighboring enemy resulting in all-out nuclear war. The song concludes with a lone human survivor standing in the rubble of a city and releasing one red balloon as a memorial that the human world once existed.

Could war really spiral out of control and threaten our very existence? Through novels (*This Is the Way the World Ends* by

James Morrow), films (*War Games* starring Matthew Brod-
erick), and poetry (*A Song on the End of the World* by Czeslaw
Milosz) we can envision how war—if left unchecked—might
lead to our extinction. God desires that such apocalyptic visions
and thought exercises will cause us to pull back the dogs of war.

Envisioning a More Humane War

As we've seen, God desires that people use their free will to end
war and the subsequent violence that tears apart communities
and countries. Sadly, humanity seems bent on war. In response,
the Holy Spirit does two things simultaneously through common
grace—he convicts people that violence toward fellow human
beings is wrong, and he affirms the desire to lessen the effect of
sinful acts, including war (Rom 2:14-15). Common grace moves
individuals to envision war in a way that shields as many people
as possible from its devastating effects. Perhaps no one has
shaped our thinking of war more than the Chinese military
strategist Sun Tzu (translated Master Sun), who wrote in the
fifth century. Not only has Sun Tzu been quoted by military
experts but also by New England Patriots coach Bill Belichick,
rapper Tupac Shakur, and even fictional mob boss Tony So-
prano of *The Sopranos*. Make no mistake about it, Sun Tzu's
The Art of War is an unflinching treatise about how to defeat
the enemy. However, it's also a book about the surprising role
compassion plays in waging war.

THE ART OF COMPASSIONATE WAR

A common theme throughout *The Art of War* is the type
of character a general should assume as he leads a nation
into war. Appealing to a higher moral law, Sun Tzu states

that virtuous generals need to exhibit sincerity, benevolence, courage, and compassion. If exhibited, then soldiers will follow regardless of the danger. However, benevolence is not merely exhibited to his army. Sun Tzu argues that even when your enemy is surrounded, leave a "golden bridge" so that rather than fighting to the death, they may choose to retreat and consider possible surrender. If they choose to surrender, they should be treated respectfully and with kindness so they could perhaps be converted from enemies to friends. Sun Tzu equally asserts that the land of an enemy should be treated with dignity as well. He's opposed to a scorched-earth approach to an enemies' cities or crops. "The best thing of all," asserts Sun Tzu, "is to take the enemy's country whole and intact; to shatter and destroy is not so good." What is most interesting about *The Art of War* is how much it advocates *not* going to war. "The supreme art of war is to subdue the enemy without fighting."[9] Negotiation, not war, was the best way to gain victory.

The idea of linking compassion and war did not end with Sun Tzu. Henri Dunant was a businessman looking for a good deal. His ambition gained him an audience with Emperor Napoleon III in northern Italy in 1859. He arrived in time to witness the carnage caused during the Battle of Solferino, during the Second War of Italian Independence. The battle involved nearly a half million soldiers, and when the two opposing armies moved on, the battlefield was littered with over five thousand dead bodies and tens of thousands of injured. Dunant was shocked. Ensuing nightmares prompted him to describe the horrors in a personal memoir, *A Memory of Solferino*. In it he articulated an idea that would change how modern warfare is managed. "Would it not be possible, in time of peace and quiet, to form relief societies for the purpose of having care given to the wounded in wartime by zealous, devoted and thoroughly qualified volunteers?"[10]

Not only did this idea give birth to the Red Cross but also a series of international meetings that came to be known as the Geneva Conventions. These crucial conventions were a series of international treaties concluded in Geneva between 1864 and 1949 to lessen the effects of war on prisoners of war, noncombatants, the infirm, and particularly children. Violation of these treaties is taken seriously and can result in prosecution in the International Criminal Court (e.g., war-crimes tribunals for Yugoslavia [1993] and Rwanda [1994]).

Though we wait for God to ultimately abolish war, we are comforted by common grace that leads diverse spokespeople like Sun Tzu and Dunant to remind us of the crucial role compassion plays in lessening the scope and devastation of war.

GOING DEEPER

Just War theory is almost as old as war itself and has been articulated by noted thinkers such as Aristotle, Augustine, and Aquinas. It seeks to determine if there is just cause for waging war *(jus ad bellum)*, and if pursued, is war humane *(jus in bello)*. Specifically, the principles of *jus ad bellum* are: just cause to wage war, being the last resort, being declared by a proper authority, possessing right intention, having a reasonable chance of success, and the end being proportional to the means used. *Jus in bello* asks, Who are legitimate targets in war, and how much force is morally appropriate? A third principle has been added suggesting that a just war will also entail taking responsibility for the devastation and long-term effect of war. Thus, nations considering war must equally consider if they have just cause, who is off-limits if they proceed with military action, and will they accept the moral, financial, and humanitarian implications of war?

Violence in Our Communities

Regrettably, man being a wolf to man is not limited to the battlefield. The streets of our communities and our very homes can be places of violence. In a disturbing passage Sigmund Freud states that we are not "gentle creatures" but rather people who often view our neighbors with the intent to "seize his possessions" and "to cause him pain." He concludes, "Who in the face of all his experience of life and of history, will have the courage to dispute this assertion?"[11]

A person spending any amount of time online or catching the evening news sees much evidence of Freud's dire assessment. Not only do soldiers need protection from enemy combatants, but ordinary people also need help in responding to physical threats. Sadly, the worldwide pandemic of 2020–2021 often brought out the worst in people. Physical altercations over mask wearing have become so common that the National Retail Federation—a group representing over sixteen thousand retailers—announced they were now training workers how to deescalate and even physically defend themselves against belligerent shoppers who refused to wear masks.[12] The training they'll receive is a powerful means of common grace. But it's not just limited to those in the sales force. As we shall see, through common grace God introduces to communities worldwide the concept of *self*-defense.

As God watched his world submerged into violence, he planted a universal idea of what disciplined and humane self-protection would look like. The scope of this idea is vividly portrayed in the ultimate reality TV show *Fight Quest*.

SELF-DEFENSE AROUND THE WORLD

What if two modern adventurers—one a veteran of the Iraq War and the other a professional fighter—traveled the world learning a new fighting system each week? Here's how the press release described this unique show: "Travel the globe with American fighters Jimmy Smith and Doug Anderson as they struggle to learn new hand-to-hand combat disciplines from top masters and embrace traditional cultures in each riveting episode of Fight Quest."[13] The show took them to China, Japan, Korea, Mexico, the United States, Israel, India, Brazil, Thailand, and the Philippines to name a few. Each country brought its own challenges and unique version of self-defense. No stunt people were used in the show—all fights were real, with the hosts having bloody noses and chipped teeth to prove it. However, don't miss the key point of the show—*every* culture developed its own style and concept of self-defense. In every place on the globe where violence sprang up, so did elaborate systems of how to defend yourself from violence.

While Smith and Anderson spent two years trying different martial arts, Charles Hackney has spent a lifetime studying the main forms of self-defense. In his book *Martial Virtues: The*

Role of Martial Arts in Character Development, he notes that virtue has always accompanied a traditional study of self-defense. The two are inseparable. "Martial arts without martial virtue," notes Confucian philosopher Nakae Tōju, "are useless."[14] As Hackney studied various martial arts around the world, he noticed five virtues common to almost all of them: courage, justice, temperance, wisdom, and benevolence. Some martial arts even require that a devotee recite a sampling of these principles before leaving a session.

DOJO KUN

Gichin Funakoshi, the founder of Shotokan karate, watched his students perform powerful kicks and punches designed to stop an assailant dead in their tracks. While pleased with their techniques, he was increasingly concerned. Would his students—particularly the young ones—understand that karate should never be used for offensive purposes or to settle a personal vendetta and the greatest virtues are humility and prudence? To drive this home, every training session ends with students reciting the "dojo kun" (a five-line summary of Funakoshi's ideals). Standing exhausted in sweat-saturated *gi*s or uniforms, the students say in unison:

Each person must strive for the completion and perfection of one's character.

Each person must be faithful and protect the way of truth.

Each person must endeavor and give full effort.

Each person must respect others and the rules of etiquette.

Each person must refrain from hot-blooded behavior.

Funakoshi believed that repeating these principles was the *most* important part of training. He would later write that karate is "not only the acquisition of certain defensive skills but also the mastering of the art of being a good and honest member of society."[15] Here Funakoshi mirrors the same concerns of the ancient Greek philosopher Plato, who wrote that the guardians of any society would turn "on the community, and each other, if their aggressive natures are not shaped and guided by other qualities, such as gentleness and a love of learning."[16]

One other note about the virtue-laden self-defense systems God seems to have spurred on by common grace. What about the protection of women—often the most vulnerable population? In the ancient world, women were often denied education and status and depended on their husbands for protection. Many first-century rabbis added to this devaluing by teaching that it was better to burn the Law than teach it to a woman. One famous saying stated, "Blessed is he whose children are male, but woe to him whose children are female." When a man tired of his wife, it was easy under Roman law to simply discard her for "moral" reasons—though the reasons did not need to be publicly stated. Once forced out of the house, the woman's options were to either beg for money or turn to prostitution—both dangerous.

Tragically, the plight of at-risk women has not dramatically improved in today's world. *New York Times* correspondents Nicholas D. Kristof and Sheryl WuDunn are the first married couple to win a Pulitzer Prize in journalism for their coverage of human rights violations in China. They have spent their entire journalistic careers traveling the world working with re-nowned activists such as Desmond Tutu to address the plight of women. Their assessment is heartbreaking.

The global statistics on the abuse of girls are numbing. It appears that more girls and women are now missing from the planet, precisely because they are female, than men were killed on the battlefield in all the wars of the 20th century. The number of victims of this routine "gendercide" far exceeds the number of people who were slaughtered in all the genocides of the 20th century.[17]

These journalists chastise the blind eye governments and community leaders exhibit in light of this tragedy. How will people look back at such callousness? "Decades from now, people will look back and wonder how societies could have acquiesced in a sex slave trade in the twenty-first century that is . . . bigger than the transatlantic slave trade was in the nineteenth."[18] They postulate that future scholars will be dumbfounded that an entire world merely shrugged as women died or went missing in astonishing numbers.

God does not shrug at the dangers facing women. His heart is evident when the Scriptures boldly state that "religion that God our Father accepts as pure and faultless is this: to look after orphans and widows in their distress" (Jas 1:27). The word *distress* connotes emotional, monetary, and physical threats. In addition to this bold directive for the church, he partners with women to create self-defense systems with them in mind.

A PEASANT GIRL FIGHTS BACK

According to legend, the self-defense system of Wing Chun was created by the Buddhist nun Ng Mui, who was a master of traditional Shaolin kung fu. She was approached by a fifteen-year-old peasant girl named Yim Wing-chun, who was the target of the leader of local bandits. The ring leader wanted to marry the girl against her wishes. To help, Ng Mui developed a system that deemphasized brute strength and punching power. Rather, the peasant girl learned to utilize short rapid punches that were meant to stun so she could run away. It worked and the bandit leader eventually left her alone. Ng Mui was so impressed by her young student she named the system after her. Today, Wing Chun is practiced by millions of women *and* men worldwide, including the late martial arts legend Bruce Lee.

GOING DEEPER

Wasn't Jesus against the very concept of self-defense? Didn't he command his followers to "turn the other cheek" when attacked? A closer examination suggests we may have misinterpreted this well-known phrase. The people of Jesus' day had adopted the idea that if you did some type of injustice to me I had the right to do it back to you. It was a bumper-sticker mentality to interpersonal disputes: "I don't get mad; I get even!" Jesus shocks his audience by saying, "But I tell you, do not resist an evil person. If anyone slaps you on the right cheek, turn to them the other cheek also" (Mt 5:39). Jesus is most likely describing a slap to the face rather than a forceful blow. "If a right-handed person strikes someone's right cheek, presumably it is a slap by the back of the hand, probably considered more insulting than a slap by the open palm."[19] Jesus was not describing a scenario where a person gets punched and then turns his bloody cheek to receive another blow. What Jesus seems to be advocating is that if you are insulted, give up your perceived right to counter with an insult. This principle, though not limited to Christian persecution, is particularly important when the insult is incurred due to a stand for righteousness (Mt 5:10-12).

When God Wages War

As I've shared my perspective of how God views violence and provides us means of mitigating it, I've been asked on multiple occasions a serious question: "Isn't the Bible filled with stories of Israel engaging in bloody wars in which they treated their enemies rather ruthlessly? Apparently, God isn't opposed to war." This thorny issue is referred to by Christian apologists simply as the Canaanite problem. However, it's not just a problem for trained apologists. When I survey my students at the Christian university where I teach, I ask them what questions they or nonbelieving friends wrestle with concerning our faith. I've done this for nearly twenty years, and the most common questions are "What about those who have never heard of Jesus?" "How can I know the Bible is trustworthy in what it reports?" "How can God be good in a world of terrorism?" "Isn't it offensive to say Jesus is the only way to God?" "What right do I have to judge the love between two people?" Over time, my students started questioning the seeming viciousness of the God of the Old Testament: "Didn't God commit ethnic cleansing when he ordered the slaughter of the Canaanites?"

The question corresponded with the release of a provocative book by atheist biologist Richard Dawkins in 2006 titled *The God Delusion*. Dawkins describes God as the "most unpleasant character in all of fiction" and compares him to a blood-thirsty Taliban chieftain.[20] Dawkins's book has sold over three million copies and spent nine weeks on the *New York Times* bestseller list for nonfiction. More importantly, his view of God has made its way into pop culture with Dawkins becoming a visible and abrasive spokesperson.

His objection to God has seemed to catch on. While speaking at an evangelistic event in Southern California, I asked the audience to describe how they view the God of the Bible. One woman stepped up to the microphone and inquired why God didn't play by his own rules. I asked her to elaborate. "Well, Jesus seems to be all about peace while the Old Testament is full of violence and gore. It seems Jesus and God play by different rules." One week later, after finishing a sermon on God's mercy and long-suffering, I was approached by a woman holding the hand of a toddler. "It's funny how we just ignore chunks of the Old Testament." "Go on," I replied. Looking down at her son, she said it was hard to think of young children and babies being killed because God wanted a particular piece of land.

Ignoring these questions isn't an option. The reason Dawkins's objection persists is that a cursory reading of the Old Testament seems to support the idea of God both decrying violence while simultaneously ordering the armies of Israel to wipe out an entire people group—the Canaanites. The argument I've been making in this chapter is that via common grace God gave us a vision for important ideas like the Geneva Convention and just war theory. If so, then how can God violate the key principles they promote—protecting civilians and children from war?

What makes the conquest of the Canaanites so troubling is not merely the Israelites driving people out of their land but also a comment by their commander, Joshua, reflecting on taking the Canaanite city of Jericho. In stark language Joshua reports that his army "utterly destroyed everything in the city, both man and woman, young and old, ox, sheep, and donkey, with the edge of the sword" (Josh 6:21 NASB). While there is no doubt the conquest of the Canaanites surfaces deep concerns about God's relationship to war, we must make sure to present the entire story. The following are puzzle pieces I present to my students and those disturbed by sections of the Old Testament that seem to promote a type of un-restrained war. Hopefully, these put Joshua's statement in context and offer an interpretation that may surprise you and your friends.

Puzzle piece 1: Blessing of the nations. In Genesis, we learn that after our collective rebellion God put into place a plan to bless all the nations through one man—Abraham. God informs Abraham that he and his family will inherit a land where God will show the world what it's like for a nation to follow divine rules meant to bring flourishing and shalom (Gen 12). However, the land is currently occupied by a people group exhibiting a way of life dramatically opposite to God's rules. Fast-forward and we see Moses—post-exodus—passing his leadership to Joshua, who in turn leads his people across the Jordan River into Canaanite territory, and the battle is on.

Puzzle piece 2: The Canaanites. The Bible gives an unflinching assessment of Canaanite culture. In Leviticus 18:25 we learn that "the land is defiled" with every kind of abomination, in-cluding temple prostitution, bestiality, child sacrifice, and wor-shiping false gods (Lev 18:21, 24, 26). While impossible to go into detail, two of these grievous actions deserve comment—child sacrifice and false religion. Under a sanctuary in the an-cient Canaanite city of Gezer archaeologists have discovered urns containing the burned bones of young children dating somewhere around the time when the Israelites left Egypt.[21] To appease their gods, young Canaanite children were burned alive! What would prompt people to do such horrific acts? One of the gods of the Canaanites was Anath, the god of sex and war, who was appeased only by sex acts done in the temple and the screams of children burning. To see an entire culture—especially young children—be indoctrinated in such inhuman culture causes us to recoil. When making this point I like to give people a glimpse into what indoctrination looks like by presenting a prayer uttered by those in the Hitler Youth League as the people of Germany prepared for the Second Great War.

OUR FATHER ADOLF HITLER

The atrocities of the Nazi regime are well-documented with the tragic extermination of six million Jews, Romani, and homosexuals. How could ordinary German citizens be persuaded by the likes of Adolf Hitler? Well, start young. In the years leading up to the Second World War, Nazi supporters systematically rewrote sections of the Bible and portrayed Hitler as godlike. Children forced into Hitler's youth program had to recite a revamped version of the Lord's Prayer offered by Jesus (Mt 6:9-11). In unison, German youth prayed:

Adolf Hitler, you are our great Führer.
Thy name makes the enemy tremble.
Thy Third Reich comes, thy will alone is law upon the earth.
Let us hear daily thy voice and order us by thy leadership,
for we will obey to the end and even with our lives.
We praise thee! Hail Hitler![22]

The offer to give their lives was sadly realized in that over five million German soldiers and civilians—many young children—died due to the delusion of Nazi leaders. The same is true with the Canaanites who had been deceived by false religion. Therefore, a primary goal of Joshua "was more about ending the Canaanites' religious and cultural practices than ending lives. The problem wasn't the people, but idolatry."[23] Pastor and Christian writer Joshua Ryan Butler offers an important clarification and metaphor: "God is pulling down the Great Wall of China, not demolishing Beijing."[24] The same is true of the armies of Israel: their goal was to dismantle the religious and military structures of the Canaanites, *not* to target civilians.

It's crucial to remember that the armies of Israel went after military targets such as Jericho or Ai, not bustling cities filled with noncombatants. There are two important facts to remember about these military targets. First, archaeological evidence "indicates that no civilian populations existed at Jericho, Ai, and other cities mentioned in Joshua."[25] Therefore, it's misguided to imagine Jericho as a bustling city full of children, mothers, and business owners. Second, these military targets were fairly small and not well-protected. "Jericho was a small settlement of probably one hundred or fewer soldiers. This is why all of Israel could circle it seven times and then do battle against it on the same day."[26]

Puzzle piece 3: God's reaction. How would God respond to the atrocities of the Canaanites? Surprisingly, he responded with restraint. According to Genesis 15:16, God was willing to wait roughly 430 years to see if the Canaanites would have a change of heart and repent. The writer of Hebrews uses an interesting word to describe the Canaanites—*disobedient* (Heb 11:31). Thus, via common grace and the conviction of the Spirit the Canaanites were aware that what they were doing was wrong. Nevertheless, they refused to change. Despite their reaction, God was willing to grant mercy. Before telling people about God's last attempt to avoid needless destruction, I share a little-known fact about the US military's air war against Japan during the Second World War.

GET OUT WHILE THERE'S TIME!

To stave off an invasion of inland Japan sure to inflict massive casualties on both sides, the US military committed to a bombing campaign designed to force the Japanese emperor to surrender. To warn the people of Japan, millions of small leaflets were dropped from American bombers. On one side was a frightening black and white picture of five US warplanes dropping bombs. At the bottom of the picture were specific names of Japanese cities soon to be targeted. On the reverse side was a message in Japanese that read in part:

> Read this carefully as it may save your life or the life of a relative or friend. In the next few days, some or all of the cities named on the reverse side will be destroyed by American bombs. These cities contain military installations and workshops or factories which produce military goods. We are determined to destroy all of the tools of the military clique which they are using to prolong this useless war. America is not fighting the Japanese people but is fighting the military clique which has enslaved the Japanese people. So, in accordance with America's humanitarian policies, the American Air Force, which does not wish to injure innocent people, now gives you warning to evacuate the cities named and save your lives. . . . The peace which America will bring will free the people from the oppression of the military clique and mean the emergence of a new and better Japan. You can restore peace by demanding new and good leaders who will end the war.[27]

The sentiment of these leaflets mirrors God's attitude to the Canaanites: *I'm not fighting you but the religious system that enslaves you, and you can experience freedom and mercy by turning toward Yahweh!* "Well, why didn't God warn the Canaanites the way the US military did?" suggests your friend. He did! Joshua sends in spies to scout out Jericho. There they encounter a woman named Rahab—a local prostitute—who shelters them. She informs them that everyone is well aware of the miraculous stories of the God of Israel coming to their aid. She states, "We have heard how the LORD dried up the water of the Red Sea for you when you came out of Egypt. . . . When we heard of it, our hearts melted in fear and everyone's courage failed because of you" (Josh 2:10-11). In other words, God had already alerted the Canaanites—not through leaflets but through miraculous stories—that they should surrender, leave, or ask for mercy, which Rahab did. And with rare exceptions most of the citizens left these military outposts and went to the hills. Like Sun Tzu, God had offered a *golden bridge* as a way to avoid destruction.

In no way am I comparing the people of Japan to the Canaanites, nor the US military to the just actions of a righteous God. The dropping of leaflets by US warplanes significantly differs from God's warning in several ways. Historians note that the dropping of leaflets may have been designed to cause mass panic to impede the Japanese military, or that leaflets were possibly even dropped after the bombings occurred. While compassion may have been a motive, imperfect governments or military leaders often have ulterior motives. Not so with God. His desire for the Canaanites—much like his love for the people of Nineveh—was that they would turn from their disobedient ways (Heb 11:31) and leave. The warnings he gave—through the conviction of the Holy Spirit, a moral conscience, and widespread stories of miracles—were prompted by divine love.

While these insights help, there is one puzzle piece that doesn't seem to fit. Didn't Joshua say his armies killed *everyone* in the city, including women and children? Yes, but did he mean what he seems to be saying, or did he merely utilize the rhetoric of his day? This last piece of the puzzle is debated by Old Testament scholars (see the following "Going Deeper"). One interesting interpretation is offered by highly respected Christian apologist Paul Copan.

Puzzle piece 4: Rhetorical bravado. One of the goals of ancient rhetoric is to provide details but do so in a way that is persuasive and definitive. We often forget that biblical writers conformed to the literary conventions of their day. They did this so their original audience would have a common frame of reference to understand the intent of their writings. Just as we might today say a sports team "blew their opponents away" or "annihilated them," the biblical writer who retells the battles of the Canaanite conquest seems to do the same.[28] Does that mean Joshua is lying or being deceitful? Not at all, explains Copan. Rather, Joshua "was speaking the language that everyone in his day would have understood."[29] Copan offers several examples of how military exploits in Near Eastern culture were reported. Consider the following:

- "Hittite king Mursilli II (who ruled from 1322–1295 BC) recorded making 'Mt. Asharpaya empty (of humanity)' and the 'mountains of Tarikarimiu empty (of humanity).'"
- "Moab's king Mesha (840/830 BC) bragged that the Northern Kingdom of 'Israel has utterly perished for

always,' which was over a century premature. The Assyrians devastated Israel in 722 BC."[30]

What evidence is there that Joshua was using this type of figurative rhetoric? Two passages are worthy of consideration. First, Copan notes that we see Joshua using this type of rhetorical bravado in saying the Canaanites were utterly destroyed and driven out (Josh 9–12), but then he utters this odd comment concerning marrying Canaanite women. "If you turn away and ally yourselves with the survivors of *these nations that remain among you,* and if you *intermarry with them* and associate with them, then you may be sure that the LORD your God will no longer drive out these nations before you" (Josh 23:12-13, emphasis added). If all women were killed or utterly destroyed, then why the warning about marrying them?

A similar tension is found in Deuteronomy 7:2-5, where God tells Israel they should totally destroy the Canaanites (v. 2). Yet God immediately goes on to offer a warning: "Make no treaty with them, and show them no mercy. Do not intermarry with them. Do not give your daughters to their sons or take their daughters for your sons. . . . This is what you are to do to them: Break down their altars, smash their sacred stones, cut down their Asherah poles and burn their idols in the fire" (vv. 3-5). Copan notes, "If the Canaanites were to be completely obliterated, why this discussion about intermarriage or treaties? The final verse emphasizes that the ultimate issue was religious: Israel was to destroy altars, images, and sacred pillars. In other words, destroying Canaanite religion was more important than destroying Canaanite people."[31]

GOING DEEPER

Not all agree with Copan's argument, including fellow
Christian apologist Norman Geisler, who asserts the
armies of Israel were justified in utterly destroying the
Canaanites, including women and children. He argues as
follows: (1) The Scriptures make it clear that the Canaanites were "cancerously immoral" and deserved divine
judgment. (2) The Canaanites had plenty of time—
hundreds of years—to repent, but did not. (3) God is
sovereign over all of life and has the divine right to take
what he gives (Job 1:21). (4) Thus, the armies of Israel
were commanded to weed out a specific culture that
could negatively pollute Israel and keep them from being
a future blessing to all nations. "No other nation before
or since has possessed this special revelation from God
or this mandate (cf. Exod. 19:5; Ps. 147:20; Rom. 3:1-2)."[32]
(5) Given the cancerous state of Canaanite society, its
children "could not avoid its fatal pollution" and therefore were not excluded from punishment. However, if
"children who die before the age of accountability go to
heaven, this was an act of God's mercy to take them into
his holy presence from this unholy environment." Geisler
concludes, "In the case of the Canaanites, it was necessary in establishing a holy nation and priesthood to
exterminate the godlessness of the city and the people."[33]

Whenever talking about this topic, I candidly explain that the
Canaanite problem remains difficult for Christians. But the
puzzle pieces I've presented seem to mesh with the view of
common grace I have presented throughout this book. No

doubt, the topic of war and God will continue to be a hot topic in today's violent world.

Conclusion

Does the idea of common grace make a difference when talking to people who have experienced violence? For the past seven years I've been training in the ancient martial art of Shaolin kung fu. As a result, I conduct self-defense seminars at local domestic violence shelters. During these trainings I often tell participants I'm a person of faith.

As I was finishing one seminar, a woman raised her hand. "What was God doing while my abuse was happening?" It was a courageous question offered by a recent survivor of abuse. All eyes turned to me. Her question is one that followers of Jesus have been asking since the formation of the early church: Where is God when evil touches us or the ones we love? I've wrestled with this question myself.

My answer that night, in part, was that he was using common grace to move the hearts of organizers to form a domestic violence shelter. The woman who ran the shelter—herself a victim of abuse—selflessly organizes groups throughout the city that minister to hundreds of women. At these shelters women receive counseling, financial help, and self-defense training. They exist because of donations from both Christian and non-Christian sources and are staffed by people who want to be there for victims. What moves these people to volunteer or give financially? God's common grace propels people to act.

I fully admit my answer is inadequate when speaking to a woman who has endured such physical and emotional pain. However, I will never forget her telling response: "Well, I

wouldn't be here without this group. You all saved my life!" The
group—made up of Christians and non-Christians alike—
immediately surrounded her. At that moment I witnessed God's
compassion, comfort, and grace in action.

Until God consummates human history with the arrival of
his fully realized kingdom, violence and war are sure to continue. We can be equally sure that whenever violence occurs
God's grace is there not only to restrain it but also to move
people to help victims recover and hopefully find restoration.

Further Reading

Paul Copan, *Is God a Moral Monster? Making Sense of the Old Tes-
    tament God* (Grand Rapids, MI: Baker Books, 2011).
C. S. Cowles, Eugene H. Merrill, Daniel L. Gard, and Tremper Longman
    III, *Four Views on God and Canaanite Genocide* (Grand Rapids, MI:
    Zondervan, 2003).

CHAPTER SIX

Is Everything Common Grace?

RESPONDING TO COMMON OBJECTIONS

"I have a question."

For the past few years I've spoken on common grace to diverse audiences. To assert that God is good and active in the midst of turmoil such as Covid-19, racial unrest, a contentious presidential election, and uncertain financial times is admittedly a challenge and has provoked thoughtful questions. The following are questions that seem to come up regularly.

Is Everything Common Grace?

You make it sound like everything is God's common grace! Give me an example of what common grace isn't. To fully grasp the nature of common grace and answer this question, we have to first understand God's disposition toward a fallen world. In chapter one, we considered an amazing statement from the earliest book in the New Testament: "Every good and perfect gift is from above, coming down from the Father of the heavenly lights, who does not change like shifting shadows" (Jas 1:17). James is asserting that God is the source of *everything* good. This goodness was displayed when God provided us with a multifaceted world and the means to manage and enjoy it. His good gifts continue to this day. "In a practical sense this means that every time we walk into a grocery store or ride in an automobile or enter a house we should remember that we are experiencing the result of the abundant common grace of God poured out so richly on all mankind."[1] Does this mean God directly creates grocery stores, cars, and houses? No, he gives us the emotional, physical, and intellectual skills to do what God does—create!

When we collectively rebelled, a fundamental change happened to us and our world. Sin made the earth *groan*, which is evidenced by hurricanes, earthquakes, cancer, pandemics, and a global climate dangerously being altered. It wasn't just the earth that changed—we did too. Our God-given abilities were used to distort God's good gifts. Thus governments turned into oppressive regimes, sexuality morphed into porn, racial diversity was twisted into racism, a foster-care system was infiltrated by child abusers who just wanted a paycheck, water and food are hoarded and used as political weapons, and on and on. Our rebellious world tumbles out of control.

Here's the good news: "Where sin increased, grace increased all the more" (Rom 5:20). In the ancient Greek language, the verb *increased* means "to be over and above a certain number or measure . . . to super-abound."[2] Eugene Peterson, the author of *The Message* version of the Bible, offers this paraphrase of Romans 5:20: "When it's sin versus grace, grace wins hands down." God didn't give up on us, and the good gifts kept coming. Therefore, racism was challenged by the civil rights movement, sexism countered by Bible-inspired suffragists, disease detected and eradicated by medical discoveries, and war made less destructive by the Red Cross and the United Nations. All of these are common grace.

What isn't common grace is succinctly answered by New Testament scholar Donald Burdick, who states, "God's gifts are marked by kindness and helpfulness, not destructiveness."[3] Anything that attempts to destroy or undo God's good gifts is not common grace, and conversely anything that attempts to restore it is. Sight, optometrists, and glasses are common grace; blindness and glaucoma are not.

How Can You Know for Sure?

To be honest, you can't prove penicillin or the Geneva Conventions are from God. Isn't this just speculation? In a sense, yes. I can't prove that Laennec's discovery of the stethoscope and the discovery of penicillin are from God. They could be serendipitous moments or pure chance. On the other hand, could it be God nudging us? Maybe. Many young evangelists, suggests Christian philosopher John Stackhouse, "try too hard to convince people that Christianity is true without first convincing them that it might be true."[4]

Those of us who teach or write about persuasion are well aware of "Monroe's Motivated Sequence" created by Alan Monroe in the 1950s. Monroe asserts that to persuade a person we must first *get their attention* and cultivate a desire to hear more. The goal of *Eyes to See* is to offer illustrations that pique the interest of listeners to hear *more*. Or, more precisely, to get our coworkers to think about curious inventions or strategies.

Peaky Blinders is a wildly popular series on Netflix. It tells the bloody story of gangs being formed in 1920s Birmingham, England, in the aftermath of World War I. One gang—the Peaky Blinders—is formed by a brilliant but cruel war veteran, Thomas Shelby. The problem is, Shelby and the Peaky Blinders are not the only vicious gang who want power. In episode after episode Shelby finds himself fighting multiple gangs at once. During one particularly bloody battle with a rival gang, Shelby does the unthinkable. He walks out in the open holding a white handkerchief. That's right, no gun, no bodyguard, no protection—just waving a dingy white cloth. And it works. He's embraced by the other gang leader, and they have a drink and talk.

Shelby borrowed a negotiation technique from pirates called a "parlay"—a temporary truce to discuss a possible settlement. *If we can talk to each other, then maybe the killing can stop!* With every reason to kill Shelby, his adversaries are duty-bound to give him safe passage to and from the meeting. What? Why in the world would pirates and British gangs honor something like a parlay? Every bone in their bodies must be yearning to take out the unprotected leader of their enemy. Yet they don't. What prompts them to be virtuous in the midst of a fight-to-the-death struggle? Self-interest or just maybe common grace?

The goal of common grace is to get coworkers' attention and provoke their curiosity to hear more. If it's possible God is partnering with a doctor, lab tech, and even a gang leader, then what other evidence is there he exists? Years ago I wrote a book with philosopher J. P. Moreland exploring reasons for God's existence called *The God Conversation*. In it we offered evidence for the existence of God and why salvation is found in his Son, Jesus. The reason I wrote *Eyes to See* is to capture our non-Christian friends' attention and interest so they'd want to hear reasons why God is real and the giver of good gifts.

Why Doesn't God Act Sooner?

Okay, if God is constantly supplying us with good gifts, then why not give us what we need to stop cancer or a pandemic dead in its tracks? What's taking him so long? This is the most difficult question, and I understand the emotion and frustration behind it. In fact, I resonate with it. If God helped us create radiation and chemotherapy to help fight cancer, then why not just give us a treatment or miracle drug that would eradicate it for good? I'm not being glib. For the past year I've watched the effects of radiation and chemo on the body and spirit of a dear friend as he fights stage 3 colon cancer. The drugs have worked, but they've taken a toll. Why can't God just inspire some medical prodigy to create a drug that eradicates the disease once and for all with no crippling side-effects? There are no easy answers, but we have some clues.

God wants to partner with us. God serves as a mentor to us as we negotiate a fallen world filled with real threats. A mentor doesn't just take over and do the work for a disciple but rather partners with them. Christian philosopher Richard Swinburne notes that God doesn't step in and fix our world for two reasons.[5] First, if he did step in, he would rob us of the real goods of coming together and working on a common goal. Yes, medical discoveries, inventions, and cooperation with others take work. But it is rewarding when we come to the end of the journey and have made the world a little better. To be honest, at times we'd rather God did all the work. I'm reminded of an old joke about Noah. A weary Noah is ushering the last pair of animals onto the ark. As two zebras start to board, God says to Noah, "Those are two females; you need to have a male and female." Noah looks up, "Can't you just change one of them?" We often want God to bail us out so we don't have to do the hard and often exhausting work. God has other ideas.

Second, if God constantly stepped in to miraculously fix the world, he would communicate that we are not co-governors. In the creation mandate we are given the unbelievable task of governing God's creation. To be given such a responsibility is both inspiring and humbling. Our track record as co-governors is spotty at best. In the movie *Oh, God!* George Burns plays the Almighty, who is portrayed as a kind elderly man. When tragedy hits a city, God is brought to trial for dereliction of duty. The prosecutor asks, "How can you permit all the suffering we see today?" God responds, "I don't permit the suffering, you do. Free will. All the choices are yours."[6] God can inspire and guide, but he doesn't force us.

Because God allows us to make our own choices, we regrettably often make self-serving ones. Imagine you are the parent of a child who suffers from a rare disease. If you are a religious person, you no doubt pray that God would provide healing. As you scour medical websites you learn that there is a drug that specifically addresses the condition your child experiences. It's a miracle. However, when you approach your doctor, you learn that while the drug exists it isn't currently being produced by pharmaceutical companies. "Why not?" you blurt out. The answer is that if the number of people suffering from a particular ailment dips below two hundred thousand, then it's unlikely to make money, so the drugs, while effective, are left unproduced and placed in a category called *orphan drugs*. It's easy to imagine how angry a parent or person suffering feels knowing a treatment exists but is not being produced. But, what about God? He's provided the knowledge and inspiration to eradicate or even cure a particular disease, but because it doesn't fit the financial goals of a corporation, it's neglected and needless suffering continues. God is willing, but sections of big business apparently are not.[7]

Another reason why we don't always get God's gifts is that we have an adversary who is bent on keeping our world in disarray. "The whole world is under the control of the evil one," John informs us (1 Jn 5:19). This means that Satan and his demons can—for a predetermined time—frustrate or slow our partnership with God. A passage that shows us the reality of this cosmic struggle is Daniel 10. We learn that the prophet Daniel is growing increasingly discouraged because for three weeks he has fasted and prayed for divine help but has received none. Suddenly, an angel appears and informs him that he was dispatched by God after Daniel's *first* prayer but was delayed because "the prince of the Persian kingdom resisted me twenty-one days" (Dan 10:13). The angel eventually broke through demonic resistance when the archangel Michael showed up to fight with him. While this passage is filled with mystery and must be interpreted with care, we can ascertain certain insights. First, while God's superiority was never in doubt, at times demonic resistance can hinder his angels and our prayers. Second, if the fight is real for angels like Michael, then we can be assured the fight is equally real for us. Third, even though Satan is inferior, he can still win significant victories.

Our ability to partner with God and utilize his common grace will be improved when we appropriate the spiritual armor outlined by Paul to the church at Ephesus (Eph 6). No doubt the first step to getting prepared for battle is to live out a biblical worldview that fully embraces spiritual warfare. "On this topic," suggests theologian Clint Arnold, "some of us suffer a double-mindedness. Although mental assent is given to the likelihood that evil spirits exist since it is affirmed in the Bible, in reality it makes no practical difference in the way we live our day-to-day lives."[8] Once we overcome our double-mindedness, we can both resist Satan and use God's gifts to better our world.[9]

Does Common Grace Limit God's Activity?

Isn't your view of common grace limiting God's ability to act or heal instantly? When people hear about my view of common grace, they sometimes misinterpret it as suggesting God always has to move in partnership with us. That simply is not true. When the Israelites were escaping the charging chariots of Pharaoh, they didn't contribute anything to the water parting. The same could be said about raising Lazarus—Jesus didn't act in concert with anyone. "Rise" was all he uttered, and life was restored. While God can act quickly and independently of us, I think he may have good reasons for going the slower route and partnering with us.

We must resist the urge to adopt an attitude articulated by a friend and colleague at my university. Dave says, "We often think God isn't in it if our prayers are not instantly answered." This attitude is fostered by our deep desire to just be done with it, be it a lingering sickness or character fault. Dave knows what he's talking about since it took years for him to overcome a severe immune deficiency that almost forced him into early retirement. Healing eventually came through hard work in the physical, spiritual, and emotional areas. Now, he's not only healed physically but is spiritually and emotionally in a place where his walk with God is flourishing. If God had miraculously taken away his immune deficiency, then Dave's growth in other areas might not have happened.

Hearing Dave's story has made me think differently about my nearly fifteen-year struggle with migraines. I've often longed for God to simply make my migraines go away! If he did, I could be even *more* productive! Do you see the problem? Getting rid of the migraines may short-circuit God's desire to address other areas in my life such as taking on multiple projects to achieve status, not wanting to disappoint people, or mentally assenting to the spiritual discipline of solitude but never getting around to it. Perhaps God is allowing my migraines to prompt me to look deeper.

"Consider it pure joy, my brothers and sisters, whenever you face trials of many kinds," suggests James (Jas 1:2). Why? It will produce endurance. Immediately remove the trial and endurance may never materialize.

Epilogue

CHANGING HOW I SEE GOD

My writing and speaking on common grace have fundamentally changed how I view God and how he acts in our world. Trying to cultivate the "seeing eye" described by C. S. Lewis helps me rightfully attribute gifts—often taken for granted—to the Giver of those gifts. Common grace has changed my expectations of how God acts.

Before I became a professor, I served with Cru (formerly Campus Crusade for Christ) for thirty years. I spent one summer in the Mathare Valley—one of the poorest regions of Kenya. We traveled to remote places showing a film version of the Gospel of Matthew. Most locations had no electricity, so we traveled with our own generator.

One night three teams went out. My team was the first to be dropped off, and we quickly set up the portable screen—big enough for a crowd of a thousand to see. And that's the number that showed up this particular evening.

Just as we were about to show the movie, a panicked student said, "We don't have the electrical cord that connects to the generator." She was right; we had a projector, screen, and generator, but no cord. A thousand people sat in the grass waiting. Many of them had never seen a movie before. This was before cell phones, and we were stranded.

So we prayed. A girl uttered, "God, we know you can do anything; you don't need electricity! We ask that you start this projector so people can learn about your Son."

Just as she was finishing, I heard the sound of a truck speeding down the road. After dropping off the other two film crews, the driver saw an extra electrical cord and backtracked to us. Barely slowing down, he unrolled the window and threw us the cord. We showed the movie and more than a hundred viewers came to Christ.

I have thought about that night for over forty years. In fact, it has in some ways haunted me. Would the projector have turned on without the generator? Could God have done that? Yes. Would he? I have no idea. Part of me honestly wishes that after the girl's prayer ended we had turned the switch *before* the truck arrived. For the projector to work without electricity would have been indisputable proof God answers prayer and decisively acts.

After writing this book, I'm at peace. Do I believe God could have supernaturally powered the generator? Yes, I do. But I'm convinced God did act that day through the driver who noticed a forgotten cord, an all-terrain vehicle, a film projector, generator, and cord that transfers power—all of which would most certainly have been seen as miracles by Christians in distant centuries. For me, God is no longer restricted to acting supernaturally without human participation—in most cases it'll likely be God and us working in tandem.

When word gets out that the prophet Nehemiah and fellow Jews are making great progress on rebuilding the fallen walls surrounding Jerusalem, a mob is formed "to come and fight against" them and "stir up trouble" (Neh 4:8). What's the prophet's response? To pray for divine protection? Yes. But then he states they "prayed to our God and posted a guard day and night to meet this threat" (v. 9). In the end, protection was provided and the building commenced. If the workers are safe and the work continues, does it matter if God did it via supernatural means or through diligent guards? The same is true for us in an unsettled world. When facing an unexpected sickness, does it matter if our health is restored solely through the prayers of family members or the attentiveness of a trained doctor who prescribes antibiotics? In most cases we'll respond to a health or financial concern by praying to God and posting a guard.

Rabbi Abraham Heschel spoke about "two ways of knowing and responding to the world: the way of reason, and the way of wonder."[1] Common grace not only provides us reasons for believing in God's generosity, but it equally prods us to see the world with wonder as we encounter good gifts daily. Once we begin to notice these gifts ourselves, the next step is articulated by the prophet Isaiah, "I will tell of the kindnesses of the LORD, the deeds for which he is to be praised" (Is 63:7). Not only will we benefit from the telling, but those around us will also learn of a gracious Provider who saturates our tumultuous world with kindness and good gifts.

Acknowledgments

No book is written in isolation. I'm indebted to J. P. Moreland for not only writing the foreword but also guiding me early in the project. Todd Pickett and Todd Hall read early versions of chapters and provided encouragement—thanks for cheering me on! To my Biola students and church families at Fullerton Free Church (shout out to Encouragement Inc.) and VOX for allowing me to think out loud with you all about this topic. Thanks to my son, Jason, who amid the craziness of his last year of law school still found time to read drafts—congrats on graduating! To my editor, Al Hsu, who is not only always available but took the time to read every page and offer insight, possible illustrations, theological perspective, and encouragement. Last, to my wife, Noreen, who always hears my scattered ideas early in the morning just as she's getting up—before coffee! You've been there from my very first publication, and your encouragement, proofing, and insight have been a constant.

Notes

INTRODUCTION: LOOKING FOR GOD

[1]"Rattle!" by Chris Brown, Steven Furtick, and Brandon Lake, Elevation Music, 2020.

[2]"Famous For" by Chuck Butler, Krissy Nordhoff, Jordan Sapp, Alexis Slifer, and Tauren Wells, Provident Label Group, 2019.

[3]The Police, "All This Time," A&M, 1991.

[4]Matt Hughes, quoted in "Matt Hughes on 3-Year Anniversary of Train Collision: I've Experienced an Awakening," *MMAJunkie*, June 16, 2020, https://mmajunkie.usatoday.com/2020/06/ufc-matt-hughes-reflects-train-collision-three-year-anniversary.

[5]Praveen Shrestha, "Ebbinghaus Forgetting Curve," *Psychestudy*, November 17, 2017, www.psychestudy.com/cognitive/memory/ebbinghaus-forgetting-curve.

[6]Philip G. Ryken, *Why Everything Matters: The Gospel in Ecclesiastes* (Fearn, Scotland: Christian Focus, 2015), 134.

[7]Sam Harris, *Letter to a Christian Nation* (New York: Vintage Books, 2008), 114.

[8]Blaise Pascal, *Pensées* 12, trans. A. J. Krailsheimer (New York: Penguin, 1966), 34.

[9]Krysten Hill, "Nothing," 2020.

1 COMMON GRACE: GOD IN ACTION

[1]Though popularized this way by Hollywood, the actual phrase uttered by James A. Lovell was "Houston, we've had a problem." Each time I've shared the illustration I get corrected, so I've adopted the popular paraphrase when

speaking. See "50 Years Ago: 'Houston, We've Had a Problem,'" *NASA*, April 13, 2020, www.nasa.gov/feature/50-years-ago-houston-we-ve-had-a-problem.

[2]Blaise Pascal, *Pensées* 429, trans. A. J. Krailsheimer (New York: Penguin, 1966), 162.

[3]"Isolation," *The Walking Dead*, directed by Dan Sackheim, written by Robert Kirkman, season 3, episode 4.

[4]Martin Buber, *Between God and Man* (New York: Macmillan, 1965), 7.

[5]Erik Ofgang, "Did a Young Igor Sikorsky Have a Vision of Aviation's Future?" *History*, August 27, 2019, www.connecticutmag.com/history/did-a-young -igor-sikorsky-have-a-vision-of-aviation/article_0c32b968-c067-11e9-94b9 -fb06cb2d82ea.html.

[6]Thank you to Kevin Lenehan Jr., a former navy helicopter pilot and legal counsel for Sikorsky Corporation, for the idea of this illustration and numbers.

[7]P. E. Hughes, "Grace," in *Evangelical Dictionary of Theology*, ed. Walter A. Elwell (Grand Rapids, MI: Zondervan, 1990), 480.

[8]Wayne Grudem, *Systematic Theology: An Introduction to Biblical Doctrine* (Grand Rapids, MI: Zondervan, 2000), 663.

[9]Our planet resides in a galaxy known as the Milky Way, which alone has over one hundred thousand million stars. And there are millions of other galaxies. James's point is clear: God's good gifts are as vast and unimaginable as the stars that fill millions of galaxies. See Elizabeth Howell, "How Many Stars Are in the Milky Way?" *Space.com*, March 30, 2018, www.space.com/25959-how -many-stars-are-in-the-milky-way.html.

[10]Paul A. Cedar, *James, 1, 2 Peter, Jude*, ed. Lloyd J. Ogilvie, Communicator's Commentary 11 (New York: Word, 1984), 40.

[11]Richard J. Mouw, *He Shines in All That's Fair: Culture and Common Grace* (Grand Rapids, MI: Eerdmans, 2001), 35.

[12]For an academic discussion of the advent of fire, see J. A. J. Gowlett, "The Discovery of Fire by Humans: A Long and Convoluted Process," *Royal Society*, June 5, 2016, https://royalsocietypublishing.org/doi/full/10.1098/rstb .2015.0164.

[13]For advice on how to share arguments for the existence of God and the divinity and resurrection of Jesus, consider consulting my book cowritten with J. P. Moreland, *The God Conversation: Using Stories and Illustrations to Explain Your Faith*, 2nd ed. (Downers Grove, IL: InterVarsity Press, 2017).

[14]Pascal, *Pensées* 449, p. 170.

[15]C. S. Lewis, *Mere Christianity* (New York: Macmillian, 1960), 21.

[16]C. S. Lewis, *The Abolition of Man* (New York: Macmillian, 1970).

[17]"Migraine Overview," *Migraine Institute*, accessed April 5, 2021, www.themigraine institute.com/migraine-overview/prevalence-of-migraines.

[18]Kathryn Jean Lopez, "Beware Governor Declaring 'God Did Not Do This,'" *National Review*, April 17, 2020, www.nationalreview.com/corner/beware -governor-declaring-god-did-not-do-this-help-us-in-our-pandemic-pain-we -need-all-the-divine-help-we-can-get.

[19]Denzel Washington, "The Mentors He'll Never Forget," *Guideposts*, January 1, 2007, www.guideposts.org/better-living/positive-living/the-mentors-hell -never-forget.

[20]C. S. Lewis, *The Joyful Christian* (New York: Macmillan, 1997), 6.

[21]C. S. Lewis, *Letters to Malcolm Chiefly on Prayer* (New York: HarperOne, 2017), 89.

[22]Sam Sheridan, *The Disaster Diaries: One Man's Quest to Learn Everything Necessary to Survive the Apocalypse* (New York: Penguin, 2013), 6.

[23]Sheridan, *Disaster Diaries*, 321.

2 GOD THE SCIENTIST: HEALING GRACE IN A SICK WORLD

[1]Rebecca McLaughlin, *Confronting Christianity: 12 Hard Questions for the World's Largest Religion* (Wheaton, IL: Crossway, 2019), 120.

[2]William Bynum, *A Little History of Science* (New Haven, CT: Yale University Press, 2012), 23.

[3]Mike McRae, "We Finally Know How Our Immune Cells Remember Diseases for So Long," *ScienceAlert*, December 15, 2017, www.sciencealert.com /long-term-memory-cytotoxic-immune-cells-explained.

[4]David's death, while tragic, is an example of how God redeems evil. Through David's death and the selfless decision of his parents to donate his blood cells for research, SCID has been significantly lessened.

[5]"Half of World Population Goes Without Basic, Essential Health Services, World Bank/WHO Report Says," *KFF.org*, December 14, 2017, www.kff.org /news-summary/more-than-half-of-world-population-goes-without -basic-essential-health-services-world-bank-who-report-says.

[6]Alexander Fleming, quoted in Katie Kalvaitis, "Penicillin: An Accidental Dis-covery Changed the Course of Medicine," *Helio.com*, August 10, 2008, www .healio.com/news/endocrinology/20120325/penicillin-an-accidental-discovery -changed-the-course-of-medicine.

[7]Bynum, *Little History of Science*, 228.

[8]For the stories of those who seek to embrace both evangelicalism and evolution see Kathryn Applegate and J. B. Stump, eds., *How I Changed My Mind About Evolution: Evangelicals Reflect on Faith and Science* (Downers Grove, IL: IVP Academic, 2016). To consider a recent rebuttal to openness to evolution see J. P. Moreland et al., eds., *Theistic Evolution: A Scientific, Philosophical, and Theological Critique* (Wheaton, IL: Crossway, 2017).

[9]Timothy Keller, *The Reason for God: Belief in an Age of Skepticism* (New York: Dutton, 2008), 94.

[10]Casey Luskin, "What Are the Top 10 Scientific Problems with Evolution?" in *The Harvest Handbook of Apologetics*, ed. Joseph M. Holden (Eugene, OR: Harvest House, 2018), 257.

[11]Thanks to my colleague Jason Tresser for helping to refine this illustration. The idea for this illustration came from Khan Academy and their informative discussion of a bottleneck event: www.khanacademy.org/science/ap-biology/natural -selection/population-genetics/a/genetic-drift-founder-bottleneck.

[12]The original document is found at the website "A Scientific Dissent from Darwinism," www.dissentfromdarwin.org.

[13]Alex Rosenberg, *The Atheist's Guide to Reality: Enjoying Life Without the Illusions* (New York: Norton, 2011), viii.

[14]"Scientists and Belief," *Pew Research Center*, November 5, 2009, www.pew forum.org/2009/11/05/scientists-and-belief.

[15]To read the full list see Michael Hart, *The 100: A Ranking of the Most Influential Persons in Human History* (New York: Citadel Publishing, 2000). Readers may be interested to note that Jesus comes in third (for self-relegating himself merely to the religious realm), while St. Paul snags the sixth spot (for serving as a key leader of the ancient church).

[16]Voltaire, quoted in Charles E. Hummel, "The Faith Behind the Famous: Isaac Newton," *Christian History*, accessed April 6, 2021, www.christianitytoday .com/history/issues/issue-30/faith-behind-famous-isaac-newton.html.

[17]Casey Luskin and Stephen C. Meyer, "Has the Christian Worldview Had a Positive Impact on the Development of Science?" in *The Harvest Book of Apologetics*, ed. Joseph M. Holden (Eugene, OR: Harvest House, 2018), 286.

[18]Reuben Westmaas, "9 Things That Make Earth the Perfect Place for Life," *Discovery.com*, August 1, 2019, www.discovery.com/science/Earth-Perfect -Place-for-Life.

[19]McLaughlin, *Confronting Christianity*, 117.

[20]Louis Pasteur, quoted in Irving A. Lerch, "Truth, Justice, and the American Way," *APS.org* 8, no. 6 (June 1999), www.aps.org/publications/apsnews/199906/truth.cfm.

3 ART: GOD'S SPOTLIGHT ON THE HUMAN CONDITION

[1]Brian Lundin, "God's Call to Artists," *Story Team*, accessed April 7, 2021, www.storyteam.org/gods-call-to-artists.

[2]Michael Kustow, "Is It the Role of the Artist to Change Society?" *New York Times,* August 2, 1970, www.nytimes.com/1970/08/02/archives/is-it-the-role-of-the-artist-to-change-society-is-it-the-role-of.html.

[3]To see Rockwell's self-portrait and learn more about the backstory, see the Normal Rockwell Museum website: www.nrm.org/MT/text/TripleSelf.html.

[4]Kieran Setiya, *Midlife: A Philosophical Guide* (Princeton, NJ: Princeton University Press, 2017), 105.

[5]Ray Bradbury, "Frost and Fire," in *The Stories of Ray Bradbury* (New York: Alfred A. Knopf, 1980), 539.

[6]Bradbury, "Frost and Fire," 569.

[7]For suggestions on how to talk about God's existence to friends see Tim Muehlhoff and J. P. Moreland, *The God Conversation: Using Stories and Illustrations to Explain Your Faith* (Downers Grove, IL: InterVarsity Press, 2017).

[8]"If the World was Ending," by JP Saxe, Arista, 2019.

[9]To read Lewis's conversion story in his own words see *Surprised by Joy: The Shape of My Early Life* (New York: HarperOne, 2017).

[10]For an in-depth discussion of Pascal's wager and its implications see Michael Rota, *Taking Pascal's Wager: Faith, Evidence and the Abundant Life* (Downers Grove, IL: IVP Academic, 2016).

[11]C. S. Lewis, *The Four Loves* (San Francisco: HarperOne, 2017).

[12]Peter G. Stromberg, "Romantic Realism and Romantic Relationships," *Psychology Today*, October 21, 2010, www.psychologytoday.com/us/blog/sex-drugs-and-boredom/201010/romantic-realism-and-romantic-relationships.

[13]James Lapine, *Into the Woods*, 1986.

[14]Stromberg, "Romantic Realism and Romantic Relationships."

[15]Dan Fogelman et al., *This Is Us*, 2016–2022.

[16]Richard John Neuhaus, *Death on a Friday Afternoon: Meditations on the Last Words of Jesus from the Cross* (New York: Basic Books, 2001), 200.

[17]Casey Luskin, "What Are the Top 10 Scientific Problems with Evolution?" *The Harvest Handbook of Apologetics*, gen. ed. Joseph Holden (Eugene, OR: Harvest House, 2001), 261.

[18]Boaz Keyser, quoted in William Harms, "America's Individualist Culture Influences the Ability to View Others' Perspectives," *Chicago Chronicle*, July 12, 2007, http://chronicle.uchicago.edu/070712/perspectives.shtml.

[19]To view Brian's stunning artwork see the *Faces of Santa Ana* website: http://facesofsantaana.com.

[20]John Howard Griffin, *Black Like Me* (New York: Penguin, 2010), 200.

[21]Kenneth Wuest, *Word Studies in the Greek New Testament* (Grand Rapids, MI: Eerdmans, 1952), 2:94.

[22]Marvin Gaye, quoted in Kenneth Womack, "Marvin Gaye's 'What's Going On': A Listening Guide," *Salon*, March 28, 2020, www.salon.com/2020/03/28/marvin-gayes-whats-going-on-a-listening-guide.

4 COMMUNICATION: LIFE-GIVING WORDS IN TODAY'S ARGUMENT CULTURE

[1]"Civility in America 2019: Solutions for Tomorrow," *WeberShandwick.com*, accessed Aril 8, 2021, www.webershandwick.com/wp-content/uploads/2019/06/CivilityInAmerica2019SolutionsforTomorrow.pdf.

[2]*Mad Max Beyond Thunderdome*, directed by George Miller and George Ogilvie, written by Terry Hayes and George Miller (Los Angeles: Warner Bros., 1985).

[3]Paul LeBlanc, "Trump Appeared to Snub Pelosi's Offered Handshake," CNN, February 5, 2020, www.cnn.com/2020/02/04/politics/trump-pelosi-handshake-state-of-the-union/index.html

[4]Reuel Howe, *The Miracle of Dialogue* (New York: Seabury Press, 1963), 3.

[5]See Ronald Adler, Lawrence Rosenfeld, and Russell Proctor, *Interplay: The Process of Interpersonal Communication*, 10th ed. (New York: Oxford University Press, 2007), 3-4.

[6]*Cast Away*, directed by Robert Zemeckis, written by William Broyles Jr. (Los Angeles: Twentieth Century Fox, 2000).

[7]Theodore Zeldon, *An Intimate History of Humanity* (New York: Harper Perennial, 1995); and his *Conversation: How Talk Can Change Our Lives* (London: Harvill Press, 2000).

[8]Thank you to my editor, Al Hsu, for this last observation about language being redeemed in the consummated kingdom.

[9]David. A. Hubbard, *Proverbs*, Communicator's Commentary 15 (Dallas: Word, 1989), 399.

[10]"Hal's Christmas Gift," *Malcolm in the Middle*, directed by David Grossman, written by Alex Reid, December 19, 2004.

[11]Judith Butler, *Excitable Speech* (New York: Routledge, 1997), 1.

[12]"The Michelangelo Phenomenon: How Your Partner Sculpts a Better (or Worse) You," *Luvze*, July 11, 2013, www.luvze.com/the-michelangelo-phenomenon-how-your-partner-sculpts-a-bette.

[13]Megan Fox, quoted in Samantha Schnurr, "Megan Fox Compares Hollywood's Criticism of Her Acting to a 'Self-Imposed Prison,'" *Enews*, August 24, 2020, www.msn.com/en-us/health/wellness/megan-fox-compares-holly woods-criticism-of-her-acting-to-a-self-imposed-prison/ar-BB18kdAQ?li =BBnbfcL

[14]Perry L. Glanzer, "The Demise of Gentleness," *Christian Scholar's Review*, October 30, 2020, https://christianscholars.com/the-demise-of-gentleness.

[15]Summer Lin, "Gender Reveal Party Sparks Massive Wildfire in California, Fire Officials Say," *Sacramento Bee*, September 7, 2020, www.sacbee.com/news/california/fires/article245543945.html#storylink=cpy.

[16]Kathryn Stockett, *The Help* (New York: Penguin, 2009).

[17]"People React to Being Called Beautiful," *YouTube*, September 2, 2017, www.youtube.com/watch?v=RZP6uJtgM34&t=152s; www.youtube.com/watch?v=kAPdf51MS2I.

[18]Norihiro Sadata, quoted in Avinash Anand Singh, "Compliments Activate the Same Part of Your Brain, as Does Receiving Money," *LinkedIn*, April 12, 2016, www.linkedin.com/pulse/compliments-activate-same-part-your-brain-does-receiving-singh.

[19]"Power of Words," *The Hindu*, April 19, 2010, www.thehindu.com/features/friday-review/religion/Power-of-words/article16371142.ece.

[20]Buddha, quoted in Jack Kornfield, *Buddha's Little Instruction Book* (New York: Bantam, 1994), 5.

[21]Murtada Muhammad Gusau, "The Value and Power of Words in Islam," *Premium Times*, April 3, 2015, https://opinion.premiumtimesng.com/2015/04/03/the-value-and-the-power-of-words-in-islam-by-imam-murtada-gusau.

[22]Confucius, quoted in Qiao Liqing and Min Shangchao, "A Study on Confucius' Views on Language Functions," *Polyglossia* 16 (February 2009), www.apu.ac.jp/rcaps/uploads/fckeditor/publications/polyglossia/Polyglossia_V16_Qiao_Min.pdf.

[23]Luther Standing Bear, quoted in Kent Nerburn, *The Wisdom of the Native Americans* (New York: New World Library, 1999), 24.

[24]Sam Harris, "Power of Conversation," *YouTube*, November 23, 2012, www
.youtube.com/watch?v=qm54pvquL2I.

[25]J. P. Moreland and Francis Beckwith, "A Call to Integration and the Christian
Worldview Integration Series," preface to Tim Muehlhoff and Todd Lewis,
Authentic Communication: Christian Speech Engaging Culture (Downers
Grove, IL: InterVarsity Press, 2010), 12.

[26]John Wesley, *A Plain Account of Christian Perfection* (London: Epworth Press,
1952), 87.

[27]For an excellent examination of how Christians can learn from the teachings
of Confucius, see Gregg Ten Elshof, *Confucius for Christians: What an Ancient Chinese Worldview Can Teach Us About Life in Christ* (Grand Rapids,
MI: Eerdmans, 2015).

5 WAR: LESSENING OUR ABILITY TO KILL

[1]Ernest Dupuy and Trevor N. Dupuy, *The Encyclopedia of Military History:
From 3500 B.C. to the Present*, 2nd ed. (New York: Harper & Row, 1986), 1.

[2]Gwynne Dyer, *War* (New York: Crown, 1985), 5.

[3]I'm indebted to my editor, Al Hsu, for pointing me in this direction.

[4]Ray Bradbury, "A Piece of Wood," in *The Stories of Ray Bradbury* (New York:
Alfred A. Knopf, 1980), 801.

[5]Thomas Hobbes, *Leviathan* (New York: Penguin Classics, 2017), 317.

[6]J. B. Phillips, *God Our Contemporary* (New York: Macmillan, 1960), 89.

[7]Alexander Moseley, "Just War Theory," *Internet Encyclopedia of Philosophy*,
accessed April 10, 2021, https://iep.utm.edu/justwar.

[8]Carlo Karges, "99 Red Balloons," composed by Uwe Fahrenkrog-Petersen,
Epic Records, 1984.

[9]Sun Tzu, quoted in Andrew R. Wilson, *The Art of War*, Great Courses (Chan-
tilly, VA: Teaching Company, 2012), disc 3, lec. 6.

[10]Henri Dunant, *A Memory of Solferino* (London: British Red Cross Society,
1947), 90.

[11]Sigmund Freud, *Civilization and Its Discontents*, trans. and ed. James Strachey
(New York: W. W. Norton, 1961), 58-62.

[12]Sapna Maheshwari, "How to Handle Fights over Masks Is the Latest Training
for Retail Workers," *Seattle Times*, October 15, 2020, www.seattletimes.com
/business/how-to-handle-fights-over-masks-is-the-latest-training-for
-retail-workers.

[13]*Fight Quest*, produced by Discovery Channel, season one introduction, DVD set, 2010.

[14]Nakae Tōju, quoted in Charles Hackney, *Martial Virtues: The Role of Martial Arts in Character Development* (North Clarendon, VT: Tuttle Publishing, 2010), 9.

[15]Gichin Funakoshi, *Karate-Do: My Way of Life* (New York: Kodansha, 1975), 101.

[16]Plato, quoted in Hackney, *Martial Virtues*, 10.

[17]Nicholas D. Kristof and Sheryl WuDunn, "The Women's Crusade," *New York Times Magazine*, August 17, 2009, www.nytimes.com/2009/08/23/magazine /23Women-t.html.

[18]Nicholas D. Kristof and Sheryl WuDunn, *Half the Sky: Turning Oppression into Opportunities for Women Worldwide* (New York: Random House, 2009), 43.

[19]D. A. Carson, *Matthew*, in Expositor's Bible Commentary, ed. Frank E. Gaebelein (Grand Rapids, MI: Zondervan, 1984), 156.

[20]Richard Dawkins, *The God Delusion* (Boston: Houghton Mifflin, 2006), 247.

[21]M. G. Kyle, "Canaan," in *The International Standard Bible Encyclopedia*, ed. James Orr (Grand Rapids, MI: Eerdmans, 1974), 550.

[22]Hitler prayer, quoted in Jean-Denise G. G. Lepage, *Hitler Youth, 1922–1945: An Illustrated History* (Jefferson, NC: McFarland, 2008), 87.

[23]Andy Patton, "Why Did God Command the Invasion of Canaan in the Book of Joshua?" *Bible Project*, accessed April 19, 2021, https://bibleproject.com /blog/why-did-god-command-the-invasion-of-canaan-in-the-book-of-joshua.

[24]Joshua Ryan Butler, *The Skeletons in God's Closet* (Nashville: Thomas Nelson, 2014).

[25]Paul Copan, *Is God a Moral Monster? Making Sense of the Old Testament God* (Grand Rapids, MI: Baker, 2011), 176.

[26]Copan, *Is God a Moral Monster?* 176. Copan notes that Israel's sevenfold march around the city was also an act of mercy in that it offered those inside seven opportunities to relent and surrender (178).

[27]"Warning Leaflets," *Atomic Heritage Foundation*, accessed April 19, 2021, www.atomicheritage.org/key-documents/warning-leaflets.

[28]Copan, *Is God a Moral Monster?* 171.

[29]Copan, *Is God a Moral Monster?* 171.

[30]Copan, *Is God a Moral Monster?* 172.

[31]Copan, *Is God a Moral Monster?* 173.

[32]It's interesting to note the commands God gave to Israel concerning cultures that lived far from its borders (Deut 20:10-18). Based on these commands (1) when walking up to the gates of a distant enemy first make an offer of peace; (2) if rejected, only the men are to be targeted; women, children and animals are to be spared after the victory; (3) all captives should be put into the service of Israel and in turn live in peace. The writer concludes, "This is how you are to treat all the cities that are at a distance from you and do not belong to the nations nearby" (v. 15). However, nations close by—such as the Canaanites— are to be driven away because they can potentially infiltrate and warp the morals of Israel.

[33]Norman Geisler, "Slaughter of the Canaanites," in *Baker Encyclopedia of Christian Apologetics* (Grand Rapids, MI: Baker, 1999), 113-14.

6 IS EVERYTHING COMMON GRACE? RESPONDING TO COMMON OBJECTIONS

[1]Wayne Grudem, *Systematic Theology: An Introduction to Biblical Doctrine* (Grand Rapids, MI: Zondervan, 1994), 660.

[2]Kenneth Wuest, *Word Studies from the Greek New Testament* (Grand Rapids, MI: Eerdmans, 1955), 1:89.

[3]Donald W. Burdick, *James*, in Expositor's Bible Commentary 12, gen. ed. Frank E. Gaebelein (Grand Rapids, MI: Zondervan, 1981), 173.

[4]John Stackhouse, "Why Our Friends Won't Stop, Look, and Listen," *Christianity Today* 41, no. 2 (February 3, 1997), 49.

[5]See Richard Swinburne, *Mind, Brain, and Free Will* (Oxford University Press, 2013).

[6]*Oh, God!* directed by Carl Reiner, written by Larry Gelbart (Los Angeles: Warner Bros., 1977).

[7]To read more about the moral dilemma surrounding orphan drugs see www.ncbi.nlm.nih.gov/pmc/articles/PMC4202455.

[8]Clinton Arnold, *Powers of Darkness: Principalities and Powers in Paul's Letters* (Downers Grove, IL: InterVarsity Press, 1992), 148.

[9]For more on spiritual warfare and how to protect our relationships, see Tim Muehlhoff, *Defending Your Marriage: The Reality of Spiritual Battle* (Downers Grove, IL: InterVarsity Press, 2018).

EPILOGUE: CHANGING HOW I SEE GOD

[1]Abraham Heschel, quoted in David Benner, *Soulful Spirituality: Becoming Fully Alive and Deeply Human* (Grand Rapids, MI: Brazos Press, 2011), 111.

About the Author

Tim Muehlhoff did his graduate work at the University of North Carolina at Chapel Hill, where he created an original four-step model gleaned from the book of Proverbs and integrated it with communication theory that sought to bring differing moral communities together to dialogue about commonalities and differences. In addition to being a professor at Biola University, he is the cohost of the *Winsome Conviction* podcast and codirector of the Winsome Conviction Project, whose vision is to *foster conversations within the church and the broader culture that deepen relationships, help to heal a fractured church, foster civility, bring compassion to a warring public square, and enrich the lives of listeners rather than tear people apart.* More can be learned about this project at winsomeconviction.com.

Tim's writings also explore the complexity and promise of marital relationships. He serves as a consultant for Biola's Center for Marriage and Relationships (cmr.biola.edu) and a regular guest on the *Art of Relationships* podcast, which is heard in over one hundred countries. For an overview of his books, sample chapters, and videos visit timmuehlhoff.com.

Also by Tim Muehlhoff

Defending Your Marriage

The God Conversation

I Beg to Differ

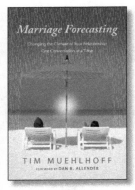

Marriage Forecasting

Winsome Conviction

Winsome Persuasion

CPSIA information can be obtained
at www.ICGtesting.com
Printed in the USA
LVHW040851020323
740746LV00003B/334

9 780830 831654